1895/f895/1295

GARDEN ROOMS

· GARDENING · BY · DESIGN ·

GARDEN ROOMS

· ROBERT · STONE ·

Ward Lock Limited · London

First published in Great Britain in 1986
by Ward Lock Limited, 8 Clifford Street,
London W1X 1RB. An Egmont Company

House editor Denis Ingram
Designed by Niki fforde

Text set in Bembo Roman
by HBM Typesetting Limited, Chorley, Lancashire

Printed and bound in Spain by Gráficas Reunidas

British Library Cataloguing in Publication Data

Stone, Robert
    Garden rooms.—(Gardening by design)
    1. Garden rooms
    Rn: Alan R. Toogood   I. Title   II. Series
    643'.55   SB419

ISBN 0-7063-6452-X

ACKNOWLEDGEMENTS

With the exception of those on pp.35, 37 and 38 all the colour photographs were taken by Bob Challinor.

The publishers are especially grateful to the following persons for allowing us to photograph their garden rooms: Mrs G. W. Williams (p. 9); Mr & Mrs R. Osborn (p. 11); Mr & Mrs A. V. Herbert (pp. 12 & 27); Mr & Mrs A. Rees (p. 28); Mr & Mrs D. Cons (pp. 31 & 63); Mr & Mrs A. Johnstone (pp. 47, 49 & 51); Mr & Mrs R. Power (p. 53); Mr C. Albert (pp. 55 & 56); and Mr & Mrs D. Hayes (pp. 59 & 60).

The publishers are also grateful to the Royal Horticultural Society for allowing us to photograph a selection of plants at their Wisley garden and to the following companies for providing photographs of their conservatories: Halls, Homes and Gardens Ltd (pp. 35, 37 & 38), and Baco Leisure Products Ltd (p. 43).

All the line drawings are by Nils Solberg.

CONTENTS

PREFACE

The garden room, also popularly known as the conservatory, combines the space of a home extension with the pleasure of the garden. Indeed, it should be a garden under glass. And a suitably chosen design, whether a small lean-to or a grand structure in a traditional style, can complement any property.

It is design, above all else, that is considered here: not only choosing a suitable style for the house and garden, but choosing accessories and furnishings to complement it.

A garden room should create the illusion that the garden extends into the room, and the secret of this is the careful choice of plants, both inside and outside.

Design aspects do not end with the structure and its furnishings; they continue when the garden room is furnished with plants. Plants should be arranged and displayed attractively, as they generally are in the rest of the garden, even to the extent of growing them in beds and borders if the garden room is large enough.

I have recommended and described a wealth of colourful and fascinating plants, for all conditions, from the warm garden room, which is used as a living area all the year round, to the unheated room for 'warm-weather living' only, but which can still be colourful all year round. I have grouped plants according to their uses in the garden room—for instance, climbers for the back wall, trailers to edge groups and staging, and pot plants for creating pyramids or banks of colour.

Affluent garden-room owners of past centuries grew all kinds of exotic fruits for the table. There is no reason why we should not do the same, on a more modest scale, so I have devoted a chapter to suitable fruit. By growing them in ornamental containers and training to various attractive shapes, there is no reason why fruits should not be as attractive as ornamental garden-room plants.

Thoughts purely on design, with no practical tips on cultivation etc, would lead the reader to conclude that the book is incomplete; but this is not so, for I have devoted the final chapter to plant cultivation; and there are many practical tips on choosing and siting garden rooms.

R.S.

1

CHOICE OF DESIGN

Considerable thought should be given to choosing a garden room, for ideally it should match the style of the house and garden. If the wrong choice is made, it can look completely out of place and be too conspicuous; but if the right choice is made, the garden room will be in harmony and blend in with house and garden.

All too often a garden room looks as though it has been added to the house as an afterthought—which indeed it invariably has, in reality, but we do not want to convey this impression. It should look as though it has been built with the house. This is not easy to achieve, but it is possible if you carefully study the various styles discussed and illustrated here, and relate them to your house and garden. If you have a traditional or period house, then the best advice is to ignore completely the modern styles of garden room. The reverse applies if you have a modern house and garden.

CUSTOM-BUILT OR READY-MADE?

It is still possible, at a very high price, to have a garden room designed from scratch by a specialist company and built on site. If you are contemplating having a house built, it would be sensible to advise the architect that you want a garden room or conservatory built into the house. A rare opportunity to do the job properly!

However, the usual trend today, with 'top of the range' garden rooms, is to invest in a modular structure, but still designed for the customer's requirements. This is the best way to ensure that the garden room is in harmony with both house and garden, for modular designs really do look part of the house.

With modular garden rooms, the manufacturers produce standardized units or modules to reduce costs. These modules are fitted together in an infinite variety of designs. The customer obtains the equivalent of a custom-built garden room for at least half the cost of a specially built model. This is why so many people today can afford a really large and attractive garden room.

Many other types of garden room and lean-to greenhouses, particularly models with an aluminium framework, are supplied in kit form, consisting of many parts, which the customer assembles on site. Of course, these are mass produced, and are far less expensive than modular structures, but nevertheless many of them are extremely attractive and add elegance to the house and garden. Timber structures are also available in kit form and are generally much easier to assemble than those with an aluminium framework, because they come in sections (usually about four main sections, but this depends on size) which are bolted together.

TRADITIONAL DESIGNS

Modular garden rooms in traditional styles, built on low walls, are enjoying great popularity today. This is not only because they look so attractive, but because many people live in period houses and consider it sensible to choose a garden room which matches the style of the house.

Very often roofs in the older styles are quite high, so they ensure plenty of headroom. They are particularly in sympathy with period city and town houses, but are just as widely used in rural and semi-rural settings.

It seems that the most popular are the Victorian-style garden rooms with their ornate windows, composed of both large and small panes of glass, the small panes generally being at the top, under the eaves. Victorian-style garden rooms are also 'decorated' with ridge cresting and other ornate mouldings.

Also available are Georgian and Edwardian styles and these are the obvious choices for owners of houses of these particular periods. These garden rooms are characterized by their small panes of glass, and the Edwardian style, especially, is rather ornate, and typically has leaded lights at the top of long narrow windows.

Sometimes the Gothic style is chosen by owners of town and city houses. The tall, narrow windows are formed into a point at the top. In the past, the windows consisted of small panes of glass, forming a pattern, but today it is possible to opt for large panes and to give the impression of small panes by the use of removable wooden traceries in panel form.

One company in the UK is supplying magnificent vaulted or arched-roof models of eighteenth-century design, with all the elegance of the palm houses and orangeries of that period. They have tremendous headroom, so large plants can comfortably be grown. Again, these buildings seem an excellent choice for period city and town houses.

MODERN DESIGNS

A modern house needs a garden room of contemporary design and there are certainly many to choose from.

Here again one can opt for a modular design at the top end of the market. The modern styles have large 'picture' windows, of square or rectangular shape, while some have curved or rounded tops, to match a particular style of house. Generally the modular garden room is unfussy, and has clean, plain lines, usually with solid walls to a height of about 1 m (3 ft).

Many people like the modular garden rooms of octagonal or half-octagonal shape, which project well away from the house. Again, solid walls to about 1 m (3 ft) are a feature of these styles as, often, is a domed or high roof.

Garden rooms with curved eaves have appeared on the market in recent years and have caught the imagination of prospective customers. The curved panes may be glass or plastic. The former is recommended, as plastic discolours after some years. These garden rooms have an aluminium framework and are supplied in kit form. Generally the glass extends virtually to ground level, so light intensity within is very good near the floor, enabling you to make good use of the floor for displaying plants. Often, too, these garden rooms have a shallow roof pitch and low ridge height, making them an ideal choice for bungalows.

Other garden rooms, which come in kit form and which have either an aluminium or timber framework, are very smart, modern-looking, box-like buildings with a low-pitched, almost flat roof.

OTHER ALTERNATIVES

Lean-to greenhouses in kit form are versions of normal greenhouses, and are often used as garden rooms. And why not? They are modestly priced and do the job well. There is a very wide range to choose from, with aluminium or timber framework, and either glass to ground level or solid sides to about 1 m (3 ft) in height. The lean-to greenhouse generally has a lighter framework than buildings sold as conservatories or garden rooms.

There are several styles of lean-to greenhouse available, apart from the traditional steeply pitched half-span roof. For instance, it is again possible to have a model with curved eaves. There is also a completely

The Eden Continental, size 3.8 × 2.2 m (12½ × 7½ ft), is a popular make and, being glazed to ground level, does not take light from the rooms of the house.

different-looking (even futuristic!) mansard or curvilinear lean-to, the roof panels of which are set at several different angles which ensures maximum light intensity within the building: excellent, in fact, for growing plants.

If for some reason you cannot, or do not wish to, have a garden room built at ground level, there is the option of an elevated structure. There are one or two companies in the UK who can design and build them, in various styles to match the house. Generally they are built on pillars, so giving space below.

People who live in penthouses and flats, and who have a roof garden, need not be denied a garden room. Provided you liaise closely with a structural engineer, or the architect of the building, and your local planning department, a roof garden can often take the weight of a garden room or a lean-to greenhouse.

So far I have not said much about sunrooms, but these are certainly applicable to this book, for they are generally very suitable places in which to grow plants, although most people invest in a sunroom to give them extra living space. Sunrooms come in various designs and are generally made of timber, in appearance more like a house extension (which is basically what they are) than a garden room. Generally box-shaped, they have far more solid walling than garden rooms, but with plenty of windows at normal height. The main reason why the light intensity within is so good, and thus suitable for plants, is that the roof is generally made from translucent, corrugated PVC.

Sunrooms generally have opening windows, but if you find that in summer temperatures become too high for you and your plants, there is no reason why they should not be fitted with some greenhouse-type ventilators, perhaps louvre vents, complete with automatic openers (see p.20).

MATERIALS USED IN CONSTRUCTION

I have already indicated that garden rooms are made either of timber or aluminium. But let's take a closer look at these materials and their pros and cons.

Timber

It is a traditional material for garden rooms and conservatories, and it has the advantage that it blends in well with the garden and is a suitable choice for any style of house, whether traditional or modern. Custom-built, modular and some kit-type garden rooms, as well as sun rooms, are made from timber.

Various kinds of timber are used by manufacturers, including the very popular western red cedar. This can be left its natural colour—which is a warm reddish brown—in which case it must be regularly treated with a suitable timber preservative; or it can be painted, the most popular colour for garden rooms being white. In this instance it will probably be supplied primed ready for painting. You will need to provide the undercoat and the topcoat, using a gloss paint suitable for outdoors. The natural colour of western red cedar is particularly attractive with the older style of house, and in rural and semi-rural areas.

European red pine is also used by some manufacturers and so, too, is mahogany, which is a very expensive timber but it has a long life. If you want to preserve the natural colours of these, they will need to be regularly treated with a clear timber preservative. I should stress that you should only use a horticultural timber preservative on garden rooms, as these will not cause any damage to plants. Paint, of course, will not harm plants, either.

Aluminium alloy

This is widely used for the kit-types of garden room, and for lean-to greenhouses. Buildings with an aluminium framework are a suitable choice for modern houses—they do not blend too well with older styles of architecture. And they do not look comfortable in country settings.

However, in recent years some manufacturers have taken to supplying 'coloured' aluminium buildings:

One could not have chosen a better garden room for this style of house for the bronze finish blends beautifully with the architecture. It's a Florada, size 2.4 × 2.4 m (8 × 8 ft).

The Banbury Classic, with its bronze and white finish and translucent fibreglass safety roofing, blends beautifully with many styles of architecture. This one measures 4.8 × 3 m (16 × 10 ft).

one can now opt for an acrylic, anodized or electrophoretic-paint finish in bronze, brown, cream or white (or perhaps a combination), and the bronze or brown finishes in particular do blend in quite well with more rural surroundings.

Aluminium alloy has the advantage over timber in that it needs no preservation treatment and it will not warp, split or rot (but neither will timber if it is well-seasoned and maintained). Aluminium is stronger than timber, and so the framework of an aluminium garden room is less bulky than a timber one.

Glass

It is highly recommended to opt for double glazing if you have the choice, for it can give up to 50% reduction in energy loss and ensure more effective temperature control, as well as muffling outside noise—particularly important if you live in a busy town or city. Single glazing is still readily available, of course, and keeps down the cost of the garden room.

Generally toughened glass, 4 or 6mm (⅛ or ¼in) thick, is used for glazing, particularly in the more expensive models, and 7mm (⁵⁄₁₆in) wire-reinforced safety glass is used by some manufacturers for the roof. Modern methods of bedding the glass in the glazing bars ensure completely draught-free conditions.

Walls

I have already indicated that the traditional garden room is built on low walls, and these can vary in height from 45cm to 1m (18in to 3ft). Many manufacturers favour brick walls (or stone walls if it is felt these blend in better with the house). Less expensive garden rooms may be supplied with pre-cast concrete walls, in various attractive finishes. One also has a choice of timber panelling for the walls. So choose (or be advised on) whichever best suits the style of your house. Many lean-to greenhouses have glass to ground level, giving excellent light intensity in this area, so you can make maximum use of floor space for plants—indeed, by skilful arrangements of plants inside and out you can create the impression that the garden extends into the garden room.

BUYING A GARDEN ROOM

There is a number of specialist garden-room or conservatory manufacturers who supply modular buildings. These companies offer an excellent service and it is best to start off by requesting their brochures and price lists, which give full specifications and illustrate many of their models. Most of these companies advertise in the gardening press, and some of them exhibit at the Chelsea Flower Show and other large horticultural shows. There are also company consultants available to give customers advice on the most suitable style for the house, and to assist with planning permission and building regulations.

There are many more general greenhouse and garden-room/conservatory manufacturers, who supply not only free-standing greenhouses but lean-to types as well. Most of these also advertise in the gardening press and provide fully illustrated and very informative brochures. Again it is possible to obtain advice on suitability and styles of buildings and on planning permission. It is possible to buy on a mail-order basis from many of these companies, and generally the buildings are supplied in kit form for DIY assembly. But throughout the UK there are greenhouse display sites, often attached to garden centres, where one can see a wide range of buildings from the general manufacturers. Not only can one compare the different makes, but also obtain advice from the site manager and his staff. Visits to your house can often be arranged, too. Manufacturers can indicate the nearest show site for their models. It does, of course, save on transport costs if you can buy from a local display site, and you can see exactly what you are buying.

Manufacturers of sunrooms also advertise in the gardening and more general press, and again informative brochures and price lists are available.

2

SITING THE GARDEN ROOM

A garden room is traditionally part of the house, with access from one of the rooms, and is either built with the house or, far more usual these days, added later. Where it is to be sited on a house wall, you must be careful to avoid hiding any existing feature of the property, or indeed obscuring a particularly fine view from one of the rooms. Of course, if you have an ugly view from one of your rooms, a garden room full of lush exotic plants could be just the type of screening you need. However, there is nothing wrong in siting a garden room away from the house, say on a garden wall. This is not as uncommon as it may sound, and it can very much enhance a garden. Suitable access can be provided between house and garden room—a substantial path, maybe in brick or stone paving slabs, which could be covered by a pergola draped with attractive climbing plants. The garden room could be set in its own patio. Of course, it will be far more expensive to lay on services, such as water, electricity and gas.

ASPECT

Although it is not essential to site a garden room on the wall of the house, it is very important to provide a site which receives as much sun as possible. Best in this respect is a south- or west-facing wall. But do not despair if the only site available is a shady or partially shady north- or east-facing wall, for there are plenty of exotic plants that will thrive in such conditions. The only thing is, you will not be able to bask in the sun. A garden room in the shade will be a bit more expensive to heat, though, for it will not be warmed by the sun.

The site for a garden room must be sheltered from wind, as cold winds result in rapid heat loss and this means higher fuel bills. If the site is not naturally sheltered, then plant a windbreak of conifers on the windward side or sides, but far enough away to ensure it does not cast shade over the building (Fig. 1). Fast-growing conifers are recommended, like Leyland cypress (× *Cupressocyparis leylandii*); certain varieties of Lawson cypress (*Chamaecyparis lawsoniana*), such as 'Green Hedger'; and *Thuja plicata*.

Try not to site the garden room between two houses, as often wind funnelling occurs in such an 'alleyway'.

Avoid, too, a site which is heavily shaded by trees. Trees are a nuisance in another way, too—the leaves collect on the roof and in the gutters, and dust and dirt is washed down from the leaves by rain, creating a lot of grime on the glass, necessitating frequent washing. The risk of falling branches should not be ruled out, either.

RED TAPE

As in almost everything we do these days, there is a certain amount of red tape to sort out. It is essential to liaise with the planning department of your local authority when you are intending to build a garden room or conservatory.

Generally planning permission is not needed, for such buildings come under permitted development. This includes extensions of up to 70 cu m (2472 cu ft) that are not on any wall fronting on to the highway.

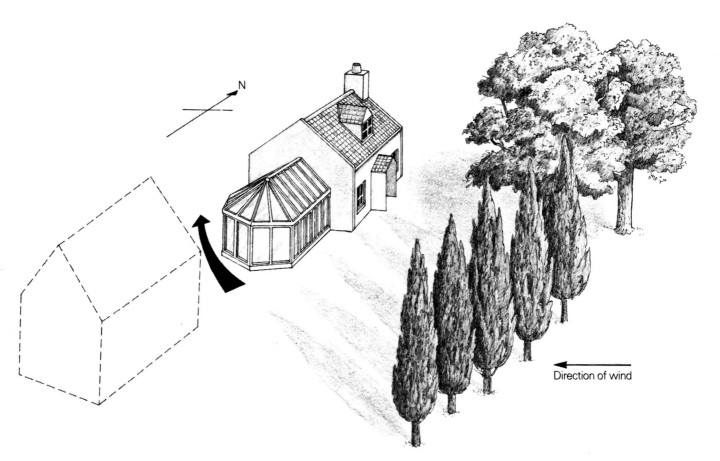

Fig. 1 A garden room must be carefully sited so that it is not subjected to cold winds, which will result in a great loss of valuable heat. The space between two houses can be a wind tunnel (arrowed) and may need to be avoided. Windbreaks can, perhaps, be planted to filter the wind. Try to avoid shade, e.g. from large trees and, for maximum sun, choose a south-facing wall.

Extensions to listed buildings need consent, though. You must check with your local planning department to find out the situation regarding planning permission in your particular area.

All garden rooms or conservatories on a house need approval under the building regulations, for the base/ foundations and the structure itself must meet with standard specifications.

The company who are supplying your garden room will provide a plan and full specifications of the building in order for you to obtain approval under the building regulations and, if necessary, planning per-

mission. When you have these contact your planning department. Many companies supply standard drawings for the base or foundations required.

All of this information must be submitted to your planning department, together with a scale plan of the site (house and garden, with the proposed garden room indicated, too). If the garden room or conservatory needs to be built over drains, manhole covers and the like, seek advice from your local authority, for building over these must comply also with building regulations. Manhole and inspection covers may have to be raised and drains reinforced.

AND SO TO BUILDING

Once you have been given the go-ahead by your local authority you can start preparing the site. The building will need a substantial base. Many garden rooms need a 10 cm (4 in) thick overall concrete slab laid on at least 10 cm (4 in) of hardcore. The concrete is thickened at the edges to a depth of at least 30 cm (12 in). Then a damp-proof membrane is laid over this, followed by a 5 cm (2 in) deep cement and sand screed (Fig. 2).

Some companies, especially those who supply lean-to greenhouses, provide a pre-fabricated base, which is simply positioned on concrete footings of a suitable depth, again laid on hardcore. But the manufacturer will advise on a suitable base and your local authority will advise on building regulations.

You may wish to build the base yourself, or employ a local builder. It is likely that the base, and the completed structure, will be examined by your local building inspector.

You also have the option of erecting the garden room yourself, or employing someone to put it up for you. Some conservatory companies undertake site erection and glazing, while others may recommend an erection service.

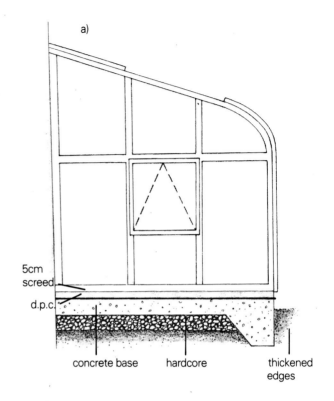

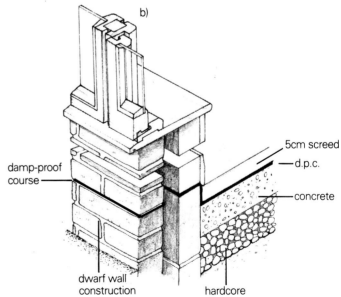

Fig. 2 Garden rooms must, of course, be built on substantial bases, complying with building regulations. The usual type of base is the concrete slab with thickened edges (a). Some garden rooms, especially modular kinds, are built on dwarf walls, the construction of which is shown in (b), but the company supplying the garden room will provide full specifications in this respect.

3

PLANNING THE INSIDE

The interior of a garden room should be planned according to its prime use. For instance, if it is to be used mainly as a living area, with plants simply as decorations, then it will no doubt resemble more the rooms of the house. If the main use is to be for growing plants, then it would be advisable to plan it more along the lines of a greenhouse.

FLOORING MATERIALS

Let us first take a look at flooring materials which are suited to the garden room for living in.

As already discussed, the garden room will be built on a concrete base, with a smooth screed of cement and sand, giving an excellent base for decorative floor coverings.

Pre-cast concrete paving slabs make a hardwearing, practical finish, and here the coloured slabs come into their own. You may like to use two colours, to give a chequerboard effect: for instance, black and white, grey and pink or grey and green. Bed them on mortar and leave 6 mm (¼ in) gaps which are later grouted, perhaps using a coloured mortar. Use non-slip paving slabs 60 cm (2 ft) square. For a very small garden room use 30 cm (1 ft) square slabs.

Traditionally, quarry tiles are used in garden rooms and they do seem to go with any style of building. They are non-slip and of a pleasing heather colour. Lay them in the same way as pre-cast concrete slabs, but leave narrower joints.

Vinyl floor tiles also make a good hardwearing and waterproof surface. There are many colours and designs to choose from, and one can, if desired, lay an attractively patterned floor. Vinyl tiles are stuck down with one of the special adhesives. Vinyl also comes in rolls, which can be laid in the same way.

Of course, there is a wide range of mats that you could use over hard surfaces. Particularly appropriate for a garden room are rush mats (being made of natural material). These could be used to cover the entire floor area, from wall to wall, laying them directly on to the cement screed. First treat the screed with a sealant to prevent dust. Rush matting is available in various colours and is hardwearing. Try not to get it wet, though, for water can mark it.

Carpeting is another alternative, and especially recommended is hardwearing cord carpeting. This can again be laid direct on the sealed screed, but you might prefer to use an underlay as well. There is no lack of colours to choose from.

If the garden room is to be used for growing plants rather than as a living area, then all you need do is seal the cement and sand screed. But if you want a more attractive finish, then again use pre-cast concrete slabs or quarry tiles. All of these surfaces will take as much water as you care to splash around!

FURNITURE

The choice of furniture for the garden room which is to be lived in is very much a personal matter and no doubt you will choose items that are in keeping with your style of garden room. However, I would like to put forward a few ideas of my own.

I feel that one should use 'garden-type' furniture in a garden room, rather than normal living-room furniture, and choose tables and chairs in cast aluminium, intricately patterned, resembling the cast-iron furniture of times past. An ideal choice for a traditional-style garden room. There is a wide choice of timber tables and chairs, in cedar or other exotic woods, appropriate for a modern setting.

Cane furniture is a good choice for the traditional garden room, while tubular aluminium tables and chairs are more suited to the contemporary building.

It has to be said that some of this furniture is not too comfortable, so if you want a bit more comfort when relaxing consider the range of upholstered garden chairs.

STAGING FOR PLANT DISPLAYS

I will recommend staging for plant displays in Chapter 4, but let us here take a look at the best places for it in the garden room. You will see that I suggest tall, tiered staging; the most appropriate location for this is against the back wall. However, if you have sufficient space you may like to have two sets of tiered staging, placed back to back in the centre of the garden room, to give you roughly a pyramid-shaped unit on which to display pot plants.

There is no reason why tiered staging should not be placed against one of the side walls of the garden room, except that it will, of course, exclude some light.

If you opt for ordinary bench-type staging, this is generally best arranged around the sides of the garden room, leaving the centre clear for furniture etc.

BEDS FOR PERMANENT PLANTS

The most natural way of displaying plants is in beds or borders. But how do we create a bed or border on a concrete slab? Simply build a raised bed (Fig. 3).

Beds can be any shape you care to make—formal, such as square or rectangular, or informal, of irregular shape. They can be created around the edges of the garden room, and even in the centre if you have sufficient floor space.

The beds can be built up with various materials, such as logs, natural stone, bricks, ornamental walling blocks etc.—whatever you feel is in keeping with the style of your garden room. Beds can even be terraced, with several levels, rather like wide steps.

It is not advisable to build beds hard up against the walls, or you will have problems with moisture. If a bed is to be built near a side of the garden room, it would be better to build a low brick wall at the back, with adequate space between it and the wall. If, however, the room itself is built on a brick wall then you will not have this problem.

Plants need a reasonable depth of soil, so raised beds should not be less than 45 cm (18 in) deep. On completion the beds will need to be filled with good-quality topsoil, light to medium loam being ideal. Better, although more expensive, is John Innes potting compost.

The beds can be completed if desired by partially sinking into the soil a few well-shaped pieces of rock.

MAKING A POOL

Pools are very popular in the outside garden, so why not consider one in the garden room? Twin pools, one inside and one outside, creating the illusion of water extending from inside to the outside, are discussed in Chapter 5.

If the garden room is built on a concrete slab, then a pool will have to be raised. If not you could have the pool at ground level, either lining the excavation with butyl rubber sheeting or sinking one of the prefabricated fibreglass units.

A pool can be any shape desired—square, rectangular or circular in a formal setting; or perhaps with gently curving edges in a more informal setting.

Fig. 3 There is no doubt that plants grow better in soil beds as they have a free root run. If the garden room is built on a concrete slab then the beds can be raised to provide a most attractive feature. The bed can be tiered or stepped and retaining materials may be natural stone, logs, walling blocks or whatever takes your fancy.

Any pool should be about 45 cm (18 in) deep, to allow waterlilies to be grown. Fish also need at least this depth of water.

To construct a ground-level pool, first excavate a hole to the shape and size required, with the sides sloping slightly inwards. While excavating, form 20 cm (8 in) wide ledges around the pool, on which to stand containers of marginal (shallow-water) aquatics.

Line the excavation with soft builders' sand, then place the butyl rubber liner in the hole and fill with water. The edges of the liner should extend over the edge on completion, and can be hidden with paving slabs or flat pieces of natural stone.

If, instead, you are using a pre-fabricated fibreglass unit, then place it in a hole of suitable shape and size and thoroughly pack the sides with soil or sand to prevent any movement. Hide the edges as suggested above.

A raised pool can be built up with bricks or ornamental walling blocks, and lined in the same way, with butyl rubber pool liner. The edges of the liner can be hidden with a final course of bricks or blocks, or with coping. Again, while building, incorporate some shelves for marginal plants.

4

ACCESSORIES

Accessories should be chosen to suit the design of the garden room, in much the same way that you choose furniture for the rooms indoors. Most accessories come as optional extras, not in the overall price of the garden room, but most manufacturers supply staging, blinds etc, to suit their particular models.

STAGING

This may be necessary in a garden room if you want to display pot plants. It ranges from the simple bench type to tiered staging on which impressive displays of plants can be built up on various levels.

If you have a timber garden room the natural choice is timber staging to match the building. Most timber staging is western red cedar, which can be left natural or painted.

An aluminium-framed garden room calls for aluminium staging, and here there is an extremely wide choice available. Much of it is what is known as 'flexible' staging—that is, it can be easily dismantled and re-arranged if you want to alter the layout of your garden room. Or it can be extended at a later date if you find you need more accommodation for pot plants.

Flexible aluminium staging consists of tubular sections which are fitted together with nylon joints to form the framework (Fig. 4). There are also shelving bars in this framework, which hold plastic or aluminium trays, or slatted timber/aluminium shelves, or a combination of both. The trays are filled with gravel on which to stand pot plants. The slatted shelves are a good choice for plants which like really good air circulation around them, like orchids and cacti and succulents.

For a garden room, the tiered staging has much to commend it, for we are interested in plant displays. The ordinary bench-type staging looks more in keeping in a greenhouse where plants are being raised, grown on or 'stored'.

AUTOMATIC VENTILATION

Controlled ventilation is essential in a garden room. You do not want the ventilators open when it is cold or windy, but you will need them fully open on a hot day to keep down the temperature. However, there is no need to be on hand all day to open and close ventilators, for there are available automatic ventilator openers which are controlled by temperature (Fig. 5). There are versions suitable for hinged ventilators and for louvre ventilators, and all are very modestly priced. I would say it is essential to have these in the roof of very high garden rooms, where the vents cannot easily be reached from the ground.

It is worth saying a little more on louvre ventilators. It may be worth your while ordering some of these (they are optional extras), for the sides of the garden room or conservatory, for they provide extra ventilation, which is much needed on a hot day. They are particularly worthwhile with garden rooms and lean-to greenhouses at the lower end of the market, which

Fig. 4 A very effective way of displaying pot
plants is on tiered staging. This allows you to grow more plants in the available
space and, of course, makes good use of perhaps otherwise unused vertical space. Tiered staging can
be positioned against the back wall of the garden room. This illustration is of a 'flexible' system—in other words, it can be dismantled and
re-assembled in a different formation, and added to, to make it longer or higher. This unit has a combination of slatted timber shelves and
plastic capillary watering trays to suit the different requirements of various plants.

are not always provided with adequate ventilation.

Further ventilation in all kinds of garden rooms can be obtained by installing electric fans, either the circulating type, which keep the air moving, or extractor fans, which create a through-flow of cool air by pushing the warm air out of the building. Fans are normally mounted in or near the roof. There is also available a solar-powered extractor ventilator, which contains a solar photovoltaic cell which harnesses natural day-light to provide power for the electric motor which drives the fan.

BLINDS FOR SHADING

It is essential to have some form of shading to protect plants and people from strong sunshine. It helps to keep the temperature down during hot weather and

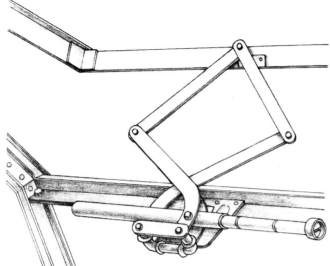

Fig. 5 These days there is no need to open and close ventilators by hand as there are automatic ventilator openers available for very reasonable prices. They can be pre-set to open when the temperature exceeds the desired level, and they close the vents again when the temperature drops. An electricity supply is not required as they are powered by natural heat.

prevents plants from being scorched by the sun. The most suitable method of shading a garden room is to install roller blinds. Some blinds are rather cheap-looking and do nothing to enhance the garden room, but others are quite acceptable, like those made from wooden laths, or from plastic reeds.

There are manually operated roller blinds available, for external use, and many greenhouse manufacturers supply them for a reasonable price (Fig. 6). However, there are also automatic systems, which provide shade only when it is needed. Of course, they are especially recommended if you are out at work all day.

One British company supplies automatic, external cedar-lath blinds which are tailor-made to fit your garden room. They can be designed to go right down to the ground if desired: especially recommended if you have a glass-to-ground garden room. The blinds are mounted on raised runners so that they do not interfere with ventilators or windows. The winding system is powered by an electric motor.

Another British company supplies non-retractable

aluminium louvre blinds for internal or external use. These are very modern-looking and a most appropriate choice for a garden room in the contemporary style. The white, perforated louvres can be tilted to any angle to exclude direct sunlight. Fitted internally in a warm conservatory, the blinds will control light only, but fitted on the outside of a cool conservatory they will help to control light and heat.

Check the gardening press for suppliers of shading blinds, or seek the advice of your garden-room supplier.

PROPAGATION CASES

An electrically heated propagation case may be needed if you want to raise plants from seeds or cuttings in your garden room (as opposed to raising in a separate greenhouse). There are many models to choose from and again you will find suppliers in gardening magazines (Fig. 7). However, bear in mind that many are purely utilitarian—that is, they are very efficient but nothing to look at. These are more suited to the greenhouse used for raising plants.

For the garden room it is suggested that a more attractive looking propagation case is chosen. There are several fairly large models around which resemble Wardian cases or 'mini-greenhouses'. (In the USA they are known as terrariums.) Indeed, this type of propagation case can double up as a Wardian case, in which you could grow delicate tropical plants which need a high temperature and even higher atmospheric humidity. Basically, such propagation cases consist of a glass or clear plastic box, complete with lid, and an electrically heated base. Some models have sliding glass doors for access.

HEATING

Most people will want to heat their garden room, not only for their own comfort but in order to grow exotic plants. Wherever possible I would recommend

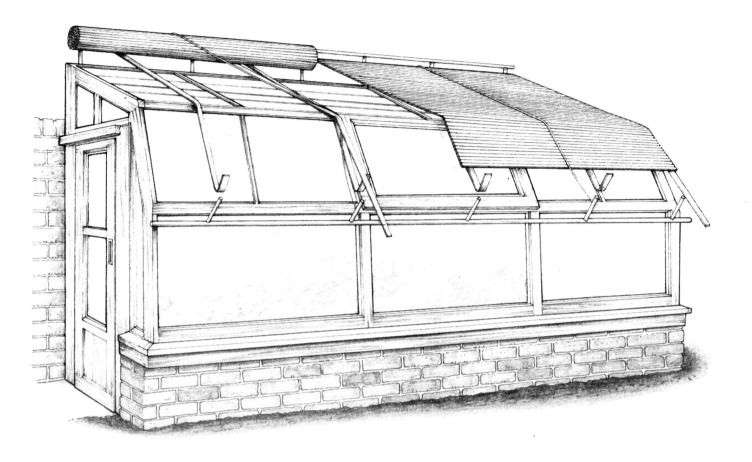

Fig. 6 Some form of shading is absolutely essential, both for plants and people, in periods of strong sunshine. There are many kinds of roller blinds to choose from, both internal and external. These are slatted wooden lath blinds, manually operated, although automatic systems are also available.

Fig. 7 An electrically heated propagating case is a very useful piece of equipment for the garden room for it allows one easily to germinate seeds and to root cuttings. Many models are available, generally with heating elements in the base, but try to choose one that is thermostatically controlled so that you can provide the temperature required by the particular subjects. Also, it will be more economical in use.

running the domestic heating system into the garden room, as this would almost certainly provide the most economical means of heating.

If it is not possible to run in the domestic system then you will have to consider an independent heating system, as outlined below. There are many companies in the UK who supply heaters specially designed for greenhouses and conservatories, and these are the ones to consider, rather than heaters for use in normal rooms, for there is bound to be some moisture around if you grow plants.

Heating with electricity

Electric heating is clean, efficient, reliable, automatic and generally convenient. It is not cheap, as we all know, but bear in mind that a good heater will have thermostatic control, so it will not be running all the time. Furthermore, you can make use of cheap-rate electricity at night (consult your electricity board).

Electricity gives off dry heat so a dry atmosphere will be created—not much liked by many plants, but there are ways of overcoming it (see Humidity, p.67). Remember that you should employ a qualified electrician to install the electricity supply.

There are several kinds of greenhouse heater. Popular is the fan heater, which consists of a small portable cabinet with a fan and heating element, and warm air is blown out, which keeps the air moving—a positive advantage as far as plants are concerned. However, do not let the heater blow directly on to plants.

Then there are tubular heaters which are installed in banks along the sides of the building—very neat and compact. They consist of hollow tubes with heating elements inside.

The third type is the convection heater, basically a cabinet with heating elements inside to warm the air. As the warm air rises out of the top of the cabinet, so cool air is drawn in at the bottom. The air in the garden room is therefore kept moving. A good choice for the large garden room.

So which type do you choose? It is purely a matter of personal choice, as they are all efficient.

Heating with gas

Gas heaters are also very popular for heating garden rooms. If you have a supply of natural gas, then buy a natural-gas type of heater. This would be cheaper to run than bottled gas. Gas heaters are basically warm-air cabinets, and are thermostatically controlled. Heaters which run off bottled propane or butane gas are portable. It is more economical to buy large rather than small gas cylinders. Ideally set up the system with two cylinders, with a changeover valve, so that as one empties the other one takes over. You will need to employ a professional gas engineer to install a natural gas supply and connect the heater to it. Gas gives off carbon dioxide, which is beneficial to plants, and also gives off water vapour which will prevent the atmosphere from becoming too dry.

Appearance and size

An independent heating system is likely to be in full view, so choose a good-looking heater. Some are purely utilitarian, the cabinet, for exmple, being simply galvanized metal. Others have a smarter coloured finish and are more pleasing in a garden room.

Size of heater is very important, for the heat output must be sufficient to maintain the temperature you require in your size of garden room. Heater manufacturers or suppliers will advise on this, if you state the size of your garden room and the temperature range you wish to maintain. Ideally a heater should have a slightly higher output than needed, to be sure that it can cope in periods of really severe weather.

LIGHTING

A garden room is very often used at night so you will need some form of lighting. For really bright illumination, necessary for reading, there is nothing to beat fluorescent tubes in the roof area. If desired these can be fitted with diffusers for a more attractive appearance.

For a more intimate atmosphere you might like to consider installing a few spotlights as well. These will give the right atmosphere for a cosy dinner party, and can also be used to highlight plant displays, especially plants which have colourful leaves or a spectacular flower display. Don't use coloured spotlights if you do not want to make your plants appear unnatural-looking. You must ensure that lighting systems are specially designed for garden-room use, and have them installed by a qualified electrician.

5

LINKING HOUSE AND GARDEN

From the aesthetic point of view there should not be a sharp transition between the garden room and the rest of the garden. One should endeavour to link the two. One can even go so far as to create the illusion that the garden extends into the garden room. This is accomplished with careful choice of plants.

BEDS AND BORDERS

If you have large-leaved tropical foliage plants in the garden room, perhaps planted in a bed or border, then hardy plants with a similar habit of growth in beds or borders around the garden room would create an effective link between indoors and out.

Hardy plants which create a tropical atmosphere include the phormiums or New Zealand flax, with their erect swordlike evergreen leaves, in the modern cultivars variegated or striped in various colours. The hardy yuccas create a similar look, as does the hardy *Cordyline terminalis* or cabbage palm, with narrow, lanceolate, greyish green leaves, or purplish in the variety 'Purpurea'.

One of the few large-leaved hardy shrubs is the evergreen *Fatsia japonica*, with glossy hand-shaped leaves. The hardy palm, *Trachycarpus fortunei,* could also be planted: this has a thick, fibrous-coated trunk and large leaves carried in a cluster at the top.

Various eucalyptus species could be grown in bush form, by cutting them back hard in spring each year. These would tie up well with any Australian and New Zealand plants you may have in the garden room.

Plants in an intermediate garden room (p.34) may be of Mediterranean origin, or at least come from subtropical climates, so in this instance the outside borders should reflect this type of climate. Provided the border is warm and sunny, try growing the more tender perennial plants and bulbs all the year round. The soil for them must be very well drained. Some particularly suitable bulbs are nerines, which produce their pink flowers in the autumn, and the eucomis or pineapple flower, which produces spikes of greenish or whiteish flowers in summer. The autumn-flowering *Schizostylis coccinea,* in pink or red, is also recommended.

Perennials which fit the bill include *Zauschneria californica,* with trumpet-shaped scarlet flowers in summer/autumn; and the wide range of grey- or silver-leaved plants, like *Anthemis cupaniana, Ballota pseudodictamnus, Stachys lanata* 'Silver Carpet', and dwarf artemisias like *A. schmidtiana* and *A. absinthium* 'Lambrook Silver'. A perennial which is not well known as yet, but which is now available from specialists, is *Phygelius aequalis* 'Yellow Trumpet', with creamy yellow tubular flowers from midsummer to autumn.

Do not forget some hardy fuchsias, too, to complement the greenhouse varieties in the garden room. Temporary bedding plants should not be dismissed, either, especially those for summer display like pelargoniums, gazanias, *Ricinus communis* (castor-oil plant), heliotrope, iresine, *Mesembryanthemum criniflorum* (Livingstone daisies), and portulaccas. These all have a 'Mediterranean feel' about them.

If you have a cool or cold garden room (one which has very little or no artificial heat), then you will be growing some of the tougher or hardier plants. It is

Inside view of the Banbury Classic, also shown on page 12. Here it is used mainly as a spacious living area.

This Banbury California, size 3.6 × 2.4 m (12 × 8 ft), has a shallow roof pitch and low ridge height, making it an ideal choice for bungalows.

sensible, therefore, from the design point of view, if the outside borders also reflect a cool climate. This is best achieved by planting a selection of alpines or rock plants in the outside bed or border. It would certainly not look right to create a tropical or sub-tropical atmosphere on the outside of the building.

There is such a vast range of alpines available today that I feel it pointless listing even just a few. The best advice is to go along to a good garden centre or alpine specialist and buy plants which appeal—with careful selection it is possible to have something in flower during spring, summer and autumn, with foliage interest throughout the winter. Plant, too, a few dwarf conifers. The scene can be completed with a few natural rocks of pleasing shape and the entire bed can be covered with a layer of stone chippings or gravel.

Coming on to water features, it is possible to create the illusion of a garden pool extending into the garden room, if you build two identical ones, one on the outside and one on the inside. Each pool will have its own walls so water will not come in contact with the building. The pools could be raised or at ground level, depending on whether or not the garden room 'sits' on a dwarf wall. The effect is most easily achieved, of course, if you have a glass-to-ground garden room.

A PATIO

Another excellent, and very popular, way of linking a garden room with the rest of the garden is to build a patio around it. Here one should endeavour to choose a surfacing material that complements the house and garden room.

In a modern setting, an appropriate choice would be pre-cast concrete paving slabs. These are available in many shapes, sizes and colours, but be wary of strong colours. Personally, I would choose some fairly neutral colour like natural stone, buff or grey, rather than, say, green or pink.

There is nothing to compare with natural stone, though, such as York paving. This is certainly more expensive than pre-cast concrete slabs but it has a subtle quality that blends with buildings old and new.

If you have an old or period property, brick paving might be appropriate and would certainly be a good choice for Victorian houses. It may be possible to match up the paving with the house bricks. Use special brick pavers, as these are hardwearing and frost resistant. There are available modern versions which could be used around a contemporary house and garden room. Bricks can be laid in various patterns, such as herringbone, or staggered like the bricks in the house walls. They are best loosely laid, rather than cementing them down, as then they are easily replaced if they become damaged, or re-laid if they sink. Lay bricks flat, rather than on edge, and leave 9 mm ($\frac{3}{8}$ in) joints which can be filled by brushing sand into them.

Gravel is a popular and economical surfacing material, suitable for most houses, from small Victorian terrace houses to stately homes. It looks pleasing whether associated with modern buildings or with period architecture. Gravel areas can also look good with artificial paving slabs, to provide a variation in texture.

Pea shingle is the type of gravel to use with modern houses, spread no more than 2.5 cm (1 in) deep, for if it is any deeper it is difficult to walk on. Pea shingle does not look right, though, with a Victorian or other older house, for it is graded, and the Victorians and earlier gardeners used ungraded gravel, which was all that was available in those days. However, one cannot buy ungraded gravel today, so various graded gravels would have to be mixed together to obtain that ungraded look.

The patio can be made to meet up with the lawn, ensuring both are on the same level to make for easy mowing of the grass. However, if gravel is used it would be better to surround the patio with small curbing stones to prevent the gravel spreading on to the lawn.

Of course, if you completely surround the garden room with a hard surface there will be no opportunity for planting. There are, however, several ways in which this can be overcome. First, you could leave areas unpaved, to use as beds for permanent or bedding

Fig. 8 Ornamental tubs and other containers are available in various materials, such as reconstituted stone, concrete, terracotta and lead. Traditional square tubs made of timber *(top right)* are extremely attractive, too. All of these can be used for growing plants, both inside the garden room and on the patio outside.

plants, as recommended earlier. Alternatively, you could leave smaller gaps in the paving, say by leaving out the odd slab here and there. Again these could be used for planting, particularly with dwarf plants and alpines of a carpeting or spreading nature. This idea not only looks attractive, but it helps to break up an otherwise large monotonous area of paving or gravel.

ORNAMENTAL CONTAINERS

Another option is to grow plants in ornamental containers, placed informally around on the patio. Again, this idea can extend the 'atmosphere' of a garden room

out into the garden, particularly if your indoor plants are grown in similar containers (Fig. 8).

There is a very wide choice of containers available, including concrete and plastic (better suited to a modern setting); imitation stone urns and vases; timber troughs and tubs which look particularly good in a rural area; and terracotta pots and containers of all kinds, which are suitable for both a period or contemporary setting. I particularly like the traditional wooden tubs—the square ones which stand on short legs. These were widely used in orangeries in the seventeenth and eighteenth centuries, but there is at least one company in the UK which supplies replicas of these tubs. They could be used for plants both inside and outside the garden room.

Any of the plants I have already recommended

In this garden room it seems as though there is one pool extending from the inside to the outside: in fact, there are two, separated by the garden–room wall. Fish in both add to the enjoyment of this feature.

The tall grassy-looking plant at the edge of this garden-room pool is *Cyperus alternifolius*. The ferny *Asparagus densiflorus* 'Sprengeri' cascades into the water, and in the pool itself are tropical waterlilies and the water hyacinth.

could also be grown in ornamental containers. Again it is a case of choosing plants to provide the right atmosphere.

A further selection of summer bedding plants could include the ivy-leaved pelargoniums, petunias, greenhouse fuchsias, begonias (both fibrous- and tuberous-rooted), French and African marigolds, lobelia, impatiens, mimulus and verbena. These could be followed by spring bedding plants (appropriate in the vicinity of a cool or cold garden room) like polyanthus, forget-me-nots, double daisies and pansies, and bulbs such as dwarf tulips and hyacinths.

Attractive containers for alpines are old stone sinks, but these are now considered collectors' items and if found will be very expensive. Instead, many people use old glazed sinks covered with a mixture of cement, sand and peat, known as hypertufa. It resembles natural tufa rock. The sink should first be painted with a proprietary PVA adhesive, and then a 12 mm (½ in) layer of stiff but pliable hypertufa mix spread over the outside, and part-way down on the inside. Plant with a selection of cushion-forming alpines, with some trailers around the edge, and finish off with a few small pieces of rock and a layer of stone chippings.

6

PREPARING FOR PLANT DISPLAYS

The plants you will be able to grow, and the extent to which you will be able to live in the garden room, will depend on the temperatures you are able to maintain throughout the year.

There are three recognized temperature ranges for garden rooms which necessitate the use of artificial heating for part of the year. Then there is the unheated garden room. Let's take a closer look at each.

THE WARM GARDEN ROOM

This will have a minimum night temperature of 15°C (60°F), with 15–21°C (60–70°F) by day, all the year round. Of course, in the summer these temperatures may be possible without artificial heating—it all depends on what our summers have to offer!

Such a temperature range is ideal for a great many plants, particularly the tropical kinds, and allows one to live in the garden room throughout the year.

THE INTERMEDIATE GARDEN ROOM

This will have a minimum night temperature of 10°C (50°F), with up to 15°C (60°F) by day. Again it is unlikely you will have to provide artificial heating in the summer. You will be able to grow a wide range of plants but conditions may be a bit too cool during the winter for living, particularly in the evenings.

THE COOL GARDEN ROOM

This will have a minimum night temperature of 4–7°C (40–45°F), with about 10°C (50°F) by day. There are again plenty of plants for these cool conditions, but winter living is likely to be out of the question. You will not have to provide artificial heating in the summer.

Bear in mind that during the spring, summer and early autumn, the daytime temperatures may well rise due to the heat of the sun. In intermediate and cool garden rooms this will make daytime living conditions much more comfortable. Indeed, during very warm weather in summer it can become too hot during the day.

THE UNHEATED GARDEN ROOM

Here, where we are providing no artificial heat whatsoever, whether or not conditions are suitable for living will depend entirely on the weather. You should, though, be able to make good use of the garden room throughout the summer months and into the autumn. Of course, you will not be able to keep tender plants in the garden room over the winter, for they will become frosted. The solution is to keep them in a warm room indoors over the winter. You should be able to have a good summer display of pot plants, such as fuchsias, pelargoniums, streptocarpus, impatiens, and others. In

This is the Bexhill Garden Room from Halls Homes and Gardens. Made of western red cedar, it measures about 4.1 × 2.5 m (13½ × 8½ ft).

the autumn you could have a display of greenhouse chrysanthemums. The unheated garden room is the ideal place to grow grapes, peaches and nectarines. There is a range of hardy decorative plants for furnishing the garden room during the winter months.

PLANTS FOR DIFFERENT TEMPERATURE RANGES

Here is a list of garden-room plants for the different temperature ranges discussed above. The majority of these are described or mentioned in Chapter 7.

The warm garden room

Aglaonema, Allamanda, Anthurium, Aphelandra, Begonia, Caladium, Calathea, Canna, Clerodendrum, Codiaeum, Cordyline, Crossandra, Cyperus, Dieffenbachia, Dipladenia, Dracaena, Eichhornia, Euphorbia, Ficus (not *Ficus carica*), *Gardenia, Gloriosa, Hypoestes, Jacobinia, Monstera, Nelumbo, Nymphaea, Peperomia, Philodendron, Pistia, Saintpaulia, Scindapsus, Sinningia* and *Stephanotis.*

The intermediate garden room

Abutilon, Acacia, Asparagus, Bougainvillea, Bouvardia, bromeliads, *Browallia, Brunfelsia, Capsicum, Celosia, Cestrum, Citrus, Coleus, Ctenanthe, Cyclamen, Cymbidium, Datura, Epiphyllum, Exacum,* ferns, *Hibiscus, Hippeastrum, Impatiens, Ipomoea, Lilium, Mandevilla, Maranta, Musa,* orchids, palms, *Passiflora, Platycerium, Rhipsalidopsis, Rhipsalis, Sansevieria, Sprekelia, Schlumbergera, Tibouchina, Tropaeolum, Yucca* and *Zantedeschia.*

The cool garden room

Annuals (hardy), *Aspidistra,* cacti, *Calceolaria, Callistemon, Camellia, Campanula,* carnivorous plants, *Cassia, Chlorophytum, Chrysanthemum, Cissus, Clianthus, Clivia, Erica, Erythrina, Ficus carica, Freesia, Fuchsia, Gerbera, Grevillea, Hedera, Hoya,* hyacinths, *Hydrangea, Jasminum,* *Lantana, Lapageria, Narcissus, Nerine, Nerium, Pelargonium, Plumbago, Primula, Punica, Rhododendron, Salpiglossis, Schizanthus, Senecio, Solanum, Sparmannia, Strelitzia, Streptocarpus,* succulents, *Tradescantia,* tulips, *Vallota, Vitis* and *Zebrina.*

The unheated garden room

Alpines, *Camellia, Chrysanthemum, Hedera,* hyacinths, *Narcissus, Prunus persica,* summer-flowering pot plants, tulips and *Vitis.*

Between early autumn and late spring conditions may well be too cool for some of your plants, unless you maintain a warm garden room, in which case they would be best transferred to a warmer room in the house for that period. Between late spring and early autumn, though, many plants, including tropical kinds, will flourish in an intermediate, cool or unheated garden room, because temperatures will be higher due to the warmer weather. Many houseplants certainly benefit from a spell in the garden room during the warmer weather, and will welcome the better light, and perhaps less stuffy conditions.

ACCESSORIES FOR PLANT DISPLAYS

As with plants in the rest of the home, most people will want to display them as attractively as possible. If plants are pot-grown, this means hiding the pots in some way, for ordinary clay or plastic pots are not particularly attractive.

Ornamental pot holders

There are all kinds of pot holders available in which pots are stood. Often, the space between the pot and outer container is filled with peat or horticultural aggregate, which is kept permanently moist to create a humid atmosphere around the plants (see p.67).

The Spacebuilder Sun Room, from Halls Homes and Gardens, comes in cedar, and there is a choice of heights, side panels, windows and doors. This model measures 4.8 × 1.8 m (16 × 6 ft).

A very modern-looking garden room from Halls Homes and Gardens. Called the Ambassador, this one measures 3.9 × 2.4 m (13 × 8 ft). An ideal choice for a contemporary-style home.

Pot holders are made from plastic, copper, brass, wood, pottery, china, and even wickerwork. The porous kinds, such as wickerwork, will need a dish in the base to catch surplus water. There are many sizes of pot holder available and, of course, many colours to choose from. I suggest fairly plain ones, rather than heavily patterned, as the latter detract from the beauty of the plants. I like soft or pastel colours, including buff, beige, cream and pale green. White also looks good, as does black and all shades of brown.

Pot holders, of course, are particularly recommended for specimen plants—plants that are being displayed in isolation.

Containers for plant groups

If you want to group plants together for display, then consider arranging them in a large container of some kind, either on the floor or on staging. You will want fairly deep containers, so that you can plunge pots to their rims in peat or horticultural aggregate, to provide humidity as suggested above.

Large containers come in the form of long troughs of various lengths, and what are generally called 'planters'. These are large deep containers, which may be square, rectangular or circular. Troughs and planters are made in various materials, such as plastic, fibreglass and wood.

Ornamental containers for permanent plants

Some of your permanent plants, such as shrubs and climbers, will eventually become fairly large, of course, and instead of keeping them in ordinary clay or plastic flower pots they could be transferred to more decorative large containers, of 30, 45 or 60 cm (12, 18 or 24 in) in diameter and depth.

There are available large terracotta pots and tubs in classical designs, and these are an excellent choice for a garden room. Also recommended are imitation stone tubs, both in modern and classical designs.

Wooden tubs are also a good choice, and these can either be stained and varnished, or painted. There are modern designs available, either circular or square; and there are classical square wooden tubs, available from one or two specialist suppliers. These are generally painted white. Originally they were used for citrus fruits, such as oranges, and they can still be used today for these and indeed other fruits, as well as for ornamental shrubs.

Hanging containers

Trailing or pendulous plants are most effectively displayed in hanging containers, maybe suspended from the roof of the garden room, or from ornamental brackets fixed to the back wall.

The traditional hanging container is the hanging basket, formed of galvanized wire. Modern versions are often made from plastic-coated wire. This type of basket first has to be lined with sphagnum moss to retain the compost, or with one of the proprietary plastic liners. Surplus water drips out of wire baskets, of course, so they may not be a good choice for the garden room.

The alternative is the modern moulded plastic type, with a built-in drip tray. Some even have water reservoirs in the base, which should be kept filled during hot weather to prevent rapid drying out. The disadvantage of the moulded plastic basket is that you cannot, unlike wire baskets, plant through the sides. The latter technique results in a 'ball' of colour if you use flowering plants such as fuchsias or impatiens.

There are other kinds of hanging container, including pots in terracotta, ceramic or plastic. These look particularly attractive when supported with macrame-work hangers.

7

PLANTS FOR DISPLAY

In this chapter I want to discuss the major groups of garden-room plants, with the emphasis on displaying them effectively. All too often plants are just dotted around haphazardly, with the result that they give a 'spotty' effect and provide no real impact. Yet it is just as easy to arrange plants pleasingly, and is far more satisfying.

I will only give cultural advice here if it differs from general cultivation, which is covered thoroughly in Chapter 9. For instance, some plants need special pruning or composts, and this sort of information is given here where applicable. I will not indicate suitable temperatures for plants, either, as all the plants recommended in this chapter are listed under temperature ranges in Chapter 6. So make sure you refer to those lists before buying plants, to ensure you can provide them with the right temperature.

CLIMBERS

The climbers constitute one of the major groups of garden-room plants, and many owners have at least one or two of the popular kinds. Many people like to see growth and flowers 'dripping' from the roof, for it gives a jungle-like atmosphere to the garden room.

Climbing plants are generally grown as individual specimens, rather than in mixed groups of plants. If you have a soil bed or border, then that would be the best place to grow them, for the majority grow much better if their roots are not restricted by containers. So much so, that some of the naturally vigorous climbers, like *Passifloras,* may get out of hand. So if you have

limited space the very vigorous kinds may have to be avoided. However, climbers can be grown in containers, potting them on until they are in large tubs.

Generally climbers are trained up the back wall of the garden room, and into the roof area if they are very tall. However, do ensure, by judicious pruning, that they do not exclude too much light. The stems can be trained to horizontal galvanized or plastic-coated wires, spaced about 30 cm (12 in) apart up the back wall and into the roof area. They should be held 2–5 cm (1–2 in) away from the walls and roof with suitable metal brackets. Alternatively, fix trellis panels to the wall on which to train the plants. Panels are available in all shapes and sizes, and in timber, plastic or plastic-coated steel. Again support them away from the wall with suitable brackets.

Less vigorous climbers can also be trained on bamboo canes of suitable height. Another idea, for pot-grown climbers, is to train the stems in a circular fashion over wire hoops (Fig. 9). These can easily be made from heavy duty galvanized wire, with legs which are pushed into the pot. Further support can be provided with bamboo canes inserted behind the hoop and tied to it. Many climbers, like bougainvillea, hoya, stephanotis and jasmine, often flower more freely when trained in this way.

Climbers which produce aerial roots from their stems, like *Monstera deliciosa* and many of the philodendrons, can be grown up moss poles, in which case they make handsome specimen plants for the garden room. The aerial roots grow into the moss and help to support the plant.

A moss pole (Fig. 10) can be used in a pot or in a soil

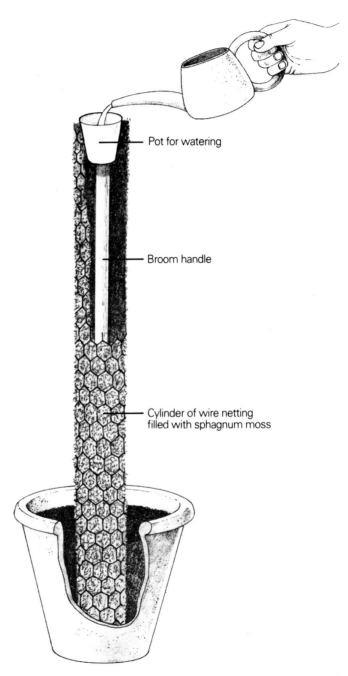

Pot for watering

Broom handle

Cylinder of wire netting
filled with sphagnum moss

Fig. 9 Many flowering climbing plants can be trained around a
hoop of thick galvanized or plastic-coated wire. This keeps them
within bounds and often makes them flower more freely. A
stephanotis is shown here.

Fig. 10 A moss pole makes an ideal support for climbing plants of
various kinds, especially those which produce aerial roots from
their stems, such as the philodendrons and the Swiss cheese plant
or *Monstera deliciosa*. The roots grow into the moss, which should
be kept moist at all times by pouring water into the pot at the top.
This is a home-made version, consisting of a broom handle
surrounded by moss, which is held in place with a cylinder of
wire netting.

bed and is very easily made. Use a broom handle of suitable length and insert this well into the soil. Place over this a cylinder of small-mesh wire netting, extending it below the soil surface. Then pack the cylinder with live sphagnum moss. Place a small pot in the top of the wire cylinder and rest it on top of the broom handle. This provides an easy means of keeping the moss moist—simply pour water into the pot and it will trickle down through the moss. If you do not use this method, keep the moss moist by spraying it with a mist sprayer. If you want to make a taller and thicker moss column, say for very large plants, then use a wooden fencing post or tree stake.

A choice of climbers

A sumptuous climber for warm conditions is *Allamanda cathartica,* an evergreen with bright yellow trumpet-shaped flowers in summer and autumn. In early spring cut back growth made in the previous season to within two buds of its base.

Varieties of *Bougainvillea glabra* and *B. spectabilis* are popular deciduous climbers, with papery bracts in purple, red or orange. In early spring cut back stems by at least one-third. Needs plenty of sun.

Clerodendrum thomsonae is an evergreen with crimson and white flowers in summer. For cool conditions I can recommend *Clianthus puniceus,* parrot's bill, of modest stature, with large red pea-like blooms in spring or summer. *Dipladenia splendens,* the pink allamanda, is a luscious evergreen, with rose pink trumpet-shaped blooms in summer. It can be pruned hard after flowering if desired. Ivies can be used as climbers or trailers. Choose from the varieties of *Hedera helix* (variegated or plain green foliage), or try the large-leaved *H. canariensis* 'Gloire de Marengo', the variegated Canary Island ivy.

Hoya carnosa, the wax flower is among the 'top ten' climbers, producing waxy white blooms in summer. It likes a peaty soil. *Ipomoea tricolor,* or morning glory, is an annual, easily raised from seeds sown in spring, with blue saucer-shaped flowers in summer. For scent, try the white-flowered jasmine, *Jasminum polyanthum,* which blooms in spring or summer. Thin out oldest stems in late winter. Everyone, it seems, wants *Lapageria rosea,* the Chilean bellflower, an evergreen with crimson tubular flowers in late summer. Because of the demand it is often in short supply. It needs peaty, acid soil.

Mandevilla laxa, the Chilean jasmine, is a tall climber with, in summer, fragrant, white, funnel-shaped blooms. It is deciduous, and best grown in a soil bed. *Monstera deliciosa,* the Swiss cheese plant, is a foliage plant which creates a lush tropical effect in the garden room. The huge leaves are deeply cut and perforated.

Only grow the passion flowers if you have a large conservatory, for they are very vigorous. Choose from *Passiflora caerulea* (blue flowers), *P.* × *caeruleoracemosa* (purple), *P.* × *exoniensis* (deep pink), and *P. quadrangularis* (light violet). Thin out oldest stems in late winter.

The climbing philodendrons are foliage plants and, like monstera, create a lush jungle atmosphere. They have very large leaves, often deeply cut. Try *P. elegans, P. erubescens, P. hastatum, P. laciniatum, P. scandens,* 'Burgundy' (red-flushed foliage), and 'Tuxla'.

Plumbago capensis is ideal for the small garden room, bearing in summer and autumn a succession of blue flowers. Prune back moderately in late winter. *Scindapsus aureus* is similar to some philodendrons, but has yellow-marbled foliage. *Stephanotis floribunda,* or Madagascar jasmine, is certainly in the 'top ten', an evergreen bearing fragrant white waxy blooms from spring to autumn. In late winter cut back main stems and side shoots.

Finally another annual, *Tropaeolum peregrinum,* the canary creeper, which produces yellow flowers in summer and autumn from a spring sowing.

TRAILERS

Trailing plants have several uses: they can be grown in hanging baskets and other elevated containers, are ideal for edging the staging, and can be highly recommended for the edges of mixed plant groups.

Baco Garden Rooms, in aluminium with acrylic bronze finish, are available in three standard lengths and two widths and any of these may be extended at a later date, using Baco extensions.

43

A choice of trailers

Foliage plants with ferny leaves make a nice foil for brightly coloured flowering pot plants, and particularly recommended in this respect is the asparagus fern, *Asparagus densiflorus* 'Sprengeri'.

Trailers with bolder evergreen foliage include the ever-popular spider plant, *Chlorophytum comosum* 'Variegatum', with grassy green and white striped leaves, and little plantlets which dangle from the ends of long stems; *Ficus pumila,* the creeping fig, with small green heart-shaped leaves; the hederas or ivies (see Climbers); *Scindapsus* (see Climbers); and the wandering Jews—*Tradescantia fluminensis* 'Quicksilver', with white and green striped leaves, and *Zebrina pendula* 'Quadricolor', whose leaves are banded with pink, red and white.

Flowering trailers include *Campanula isophylla,* the trailing bellflower, which produces a succession of blue starry flowers in summer and autumn; any of the trailing varieties of greenhouse fuchsias, which flower throughout summer; and varieties of the ivy-leaved pelargonium, *Pelargonium peltatum,* also summer flowering. New plants of all of these should be raised from cuttings annually, as young plants are best.

EPIPHYTIC PLANTS

A good way of displaying epiphytic or tree-dwelling plants is to mount them on a tree branch—indeed, some absolutely refuse to grow in pots, particularly the air plants or atmospheric tillandsias. In any case, this is the most natural way of displaying such plants and creates an impressive feature in the garden room. In the wild, the plants absorb the moisture and foods they need from the moist air around them, and from rainwater which runs down the tree trunks. Under cultivation we provide water by spraying the tree and the plants—daily in very warm weather, or maybe as little as once a week in cool conditions. Feeding can be accomplished by monthly foliar feeding in the summer, using a liquid fertilizer at quarter-strength.

Always use rainwater or soft water for epiphytes as they dislike hard or alkaline water.

Find a well-branched tree branch of suitable height and either cement it in a clay pot of suitable size, or insert it firmly in a soil bed (Fig. 11).

There are various ways of securing plants to the tree branch. If they are supplied in pots, remove the pots, tease away some of the compost, wrap the roots with sphagnum moss and wire the plant to the branch, ideally nestling it in a crotch. Use thin plastic-coated or copper wire, and do not tie too tightly. The air plants, or atmospheric tillandsias, must not have any compost or moss surrounding their roots (if indeed they have any): simply wedge them in crotches, or gently tie them to a branch.

A choice of epiphytes

Many of the bromeliads (relations of the pineapple) are the first choice. These include the atmospheric tillandsias, already mentioned, plus such plants as *Vriesia splendens,* with brown-banded leaves; *Guzmania lingulata,* orange flowers; *Nidularium fulgens,* red and violet flowers; *Tillandsia cyanea,* pink and blue flowers; and the popular urn plant, *Aechmea fasciata,* with grey leaves and blue and pink flowers.

Other epiphytic plants include many of the orchids (check their habit before buying); the staghorn fern, *Platycerium bifurcatum,* with antler-like fronds; and the forest cacti, like orchid cacti or epiphyllums, rhipsalidopsis, rhipsalis, and schlumbergeras (including the popular Christmas cactus).

SHORT-TERM POT PLANTS

This group embraces some of the most popular plants for providing colour in the garden room. They are called short-term plants because they are discarded when their display is over, new plants being raised each year. The majority are raised from seeds sown in

This tall L-shaped garden room was designed and built privately, and extends to the first–floor level of the house. The construction is timber, with aluminium glazing bars for the roof.

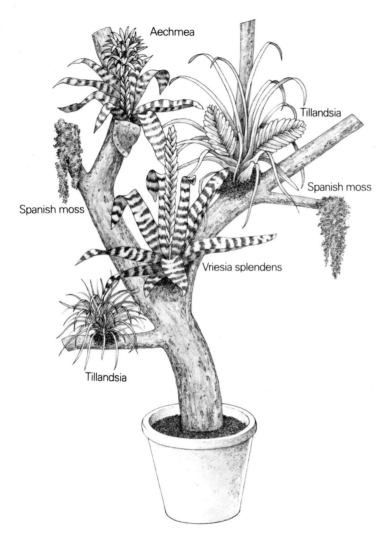

Fig. 11 The best way to grow epiphytic or tree-dwelling plants, like many of the bromeliads (some of which are shown here), is on a plant tree. The plants can be tied on to the tree, or planted in little pockets formed from a piece of bark nailed to the tree. Watering is accomplished by spraying the plants and the tree with water. A plant tree is made from a section of tree or from a suitably branched tree branch. It can, of course, be any size desired, and in this illustration it has been cemented into a clay flower pot.

Fig. 12 Plants should ideally be displayed in groups as then they create more impact and their own micro-climate. There are many large floor containers or 'planters' available for displaying plants. The planter can be filled with peat and the pots plunged to their rims in this. It should be kept moist, when it will result in a moist atmosphere being created around the plants, which is particularly desirable for many tropical kinds in warm conditions. You must ensure that all plants need the same conditions. Do not mix those, for instance, which need warm and moist conditions, with those which need cool and dry conditions.

spring, but greenhouse chrysanthemums are propagated from cuttings in early spring.

Pot plants are generally displayed on staging; aim to create some attractive groups, rather than placing plants haphazardly. Group together flowering as well as foliage plants. To give you an idea of what I mean, try arranging foliage plants like asparagus ferns, grevilleas and hederas among flowering pot plants like primulas, senecios, calceolarias, capsicums and solanums. Such foliage plants also look good among spring-flowering bulbs, such as daffodils, hyacinths and tulips.

For a summer display I like to arrange variegated abutilons, chlorophytums and coleus with flowering

A half–octagonal design from Room Outside Ltd. The curved tops to the windows echo those of the ground floor of the house, and the patio forms a link with the garden. Size approximately 4.8 × 4.5 m (16 × 15 ft).

plants such as fuchsias, pelargoniums, streptocarpus, celosias, impatiens, browallias and exacums.

You may wish to arrange pot plants in large troughs or planters on the floor (Fig. 12). Here, aim to create an attractively shaped group. For instance, if you are arranging plants in a long trough, I suggest a triangular shape: place some tall plants in the centre, and gradually grade down to each end with lower-growing plants, finishing off at the ends, and at the front, with trailing plants. Such an arrangement is suitable for placing against a wall of the garden room.

If you are arranging plants in, say, a large square planter, perhaps as a centrepiece for the garden room, then go for a pyramid shape. In other words, arrange some tall plants in the centre, and gradually grade down to each side with shorter plants, finishing off at the edges with trailing plants.

A choice of short-term pot plants

I feel that not enough use is made of the hardy annuals for the cool or unheated garden room. Subjects like clarkia, cornflower (Centaurea cyanus), Echium plantagineum, godetia and Lavatera trimestris make excellent pot plants for flowering in the spring. Seeds should be sown in late summer and the plants grown very cool. Other indispensable spring-flowering pot plants include calceolaria, with pouched flowers in brilliant colours; Primula obconica and P. malacoides, in many colours; and Senecio × hybridus, or cinerarias, with large heads of daisy-like flowers in many shades.

For summer colour try browallias in blue or white; the feathery-flowered Celosia plumosa, in shades of red, yellow and apricot; the lavender Exacum affine; impatiens (busy lizzies) in a wide range of colours; and schizanthus, with multi-coloured orchid-like blooms.

For autumn and winter the coloured berries of capsicums or ornamental peppers, and of solanums or winter cherries, are always welcome, as, of course, are the blooms of the greenhouse chrysanthemums, whether tall varieties or the dwarf charm chrysanthemums. If you have the space for the long stems, which are trained downwards, try the cascade chrysanthemums. The last two are raised from seeds sown in late winter.

Foliage pot plants can include the ever-popular coleus, and the polka dot plant, Hypoestes sanguinolenta, with pink-splashed leaves—fairly new, but has quickly risen in the popularity charts.

PERMANENT FLOWERING AND FOLIAGE PLANTS

There is a wealth of plants which are treated as permanent residents of the garden room. Whether it is warm, intermediate or cool, there is a good choice of shrubs, perennials and the like.

There is no doubt that the best way to display these is to plant them in a soil bed or border, as here they look completely natural and, of course, will make better growth. But they may also be grown in pots or tubs, and displayed either on the floor or on the staging, depending on their size.

Again, do try to arrange the plants tastefully, combining flowering and foliage kinds, as I outlined in the section on short-term pot plants. The coloured photographs give a good idea of how to arrange plants effectively. Use plenty of trailing kinds, too, at the edges and front of groups. In beds, small perennial plants can be planted among larger shrubs. Aim for contrasts in flower and foliage colour, shape and texture.

A choice of flowering plants

ABUTILON. Large shrubs with bell-shaped flowers in summer, in shades of red, yellow or orange. Prune hard back in early spring.

ACACIA. Wattle, A. baileyana, evergreen shrub, yellow flowers in spring. Can cut back after flowering.

An interior view of the garden room shown on page 47. It is used by the owners as much for plants as for living in.

ANTHURIUM. Evergreen perennials, with scarlet or orange-red spathes. Peaty compost preferred.

APHELANDRA. The zebra plant, *A. squarrosa* 'Louisae', has yellow flower heads and white-striped, evergreen foliage.

BEGONIA. For winter flowering try 'Gloire de Lorraine' and 'Elatior' hybrids. *B. corallina* has pink blooms from spring to autumn.

BOUVARDIA. *B.* × *domestica* is a small evergreen shrub with scarlet blooms in summer. Prune back in early spring.

BRUNFELSIA. *B. calycina* is an evergreen shrub with large blue-purple flowers in summer.

CALLISTEMON. The bottle brush, available in several species, is a small evergreen shrub with red brush-like flowers in summer. Acid compost needed.

CAMELLIA. Evergreen shrubs with flowers in shades of red, pink or white, in winter/spring. Need acid compost; stand plants outdoors after flowering if in pots.

CASSIA. *C. corymbosa* is a small evergreen shrub with yellow pea-like flowers in summer/autumn. Prune back in late winter.

CESTRUM. Tall shrubs, ideal for training to the back wall. Prune out old stems in late winter; reduce height if necessary. There are several species, with red, pink or orange blooms in summer or autumn.

CITRUS. The calamondin, *C. microcarpa*, is a small shrub with scented white blooms and tiny oranges.

CLIVIA. The evergreen perennial, *C. miniata*, has orange blooms in spring/summer.

CROSSANDRA. *C. infundibuliformis* is an evergreen shrub of modest size with orange-red blooms in summer. Prune back by half in early spring.

CYMBIDIUM. The cymbidium orchids are easily grown in the cool garden room, and flower in winter and spring.

The miniatures take up little space. Use a compost of equal parts bark and peat.

DATURA. Tall evergreen or deciduous shrubs for the larger garden room, with white or orange trumpet-shaped blooms in summer. Prune almost to ground level in late winter.

ERICA. The heather, *Erica* × *hyemalis*, is a small shrub with pink and white blooms in autumn/winter. All the ericas need acid, peat-based compost.

ERYTHRINA. *E. crista-galli*, the coral tree, is a deciduous shrub with scarlet pea-like flowers in summer. Keep virtually dry in winter, and cut all stems almost to soil level in spring.

EUPHORBIA. The poinsettia, *Euphorbia pulcherrima*, has large scarlet bracts in winter, but it is not easy to get it to flower again.

FUCHSIA. Deciduous shrubs, blooming all summer. Can be grown as bushes, standards or fan shapes against the back wall. Plants can be kept, or raised anew each year from cuttings. Prune back old plants in early spring.

GARDENIA. The Cape jasmine, *G. jasminoides*, is an evergreen shrub with scented white flowers in summer/autumn. Prune back by half after flowering.

GERBERA. The Barberton daisy, *Gerbera jamesonii*, is a perennial with yellow, orange or pink daisy flowers in spring and summer. There is also a dwarf variety called 'Happipot'.

HIBISCUS. Cultivars of *Hibiscus rosa-sinensis* produce their large flared flowers in summer. Colours include red, pink, yellow, orange and white. They are deciduous shrubs and can be pruned hard in late winter.

HYDRANGEA. Varieties of the garden hydrangea, *H. macrophylla*, produce their large mop-headed blooms in spring in the cool garden room. The blooms may be pink or blue (the latter in acid compost). Best to raise new plants each year by taking cuttings in spring.

In this garden room, also shown on page 47, there is a wealth of interesting plants, like a purple-leaved aeonium and a boldly veined anthurium. The flowers include begonias and gloxinias.

JACOBINIA. Evergreen shrubs: *J. carnea* is bright pink, and *J. pauciflora* is scarlet; both bloom in summer. Hard prune after flowering.

LANTANA. Lantana camara is a small shrub with a long succession of yellow flowers in summer and autumn. Hard prune established plants in early spring.

NERIUM. The oleander, *Nerium oleander,* is an evergreen shrub with pink, red or purple-red flowers in summer and autumn.

PELARGONIUM. The regal pelargonium, varieties of *P. domesticum,* flower in summer and come in shades of red, pink, purple, mauve and white. Best to raise new plants each year from cuttings taken in late summer.

PUNICA. The dwarf pomegranate, *Punica granatum* 'Nana', is a small bushy deciduous shrub with scarlet blooms in summer.

RHODODENDRON. The Indian azalea, cultivars of *R. simsii,* bloom in autumn and winter. Shades of pink, red, white etc. A small evergreen shrub, needing acid compost.

SAINTPAULIA. African violets are small evergreen perennials, with a long season of flowering. Colours include blue, purple, violet, pink, red and white. Grow in peat-based compost, in shallow pots.

SPARMANNIA. The African hemp, *S. africana,* is a large evergreen shrub, with big leaves and white blooms in spring and summer. Pot culture restricts its size.

STRELITZIA. The bird of paradise flower, *S. reginae,* has large striking orange and blue flowers in summer. It is an evergreen perennial with large banana-like leaves. Needs plenty of sun.

STREPTOCARPUS. The Cape primroses are evergreen perennials, flowering in summer, purple-blue in the variety 'Constant Nymph', various colours in the John Innes hybrids.

TIBOUCHINA. The glory bush, *T. semidecandra,* is an evergreen shrub with blue-purple, saucer-shaped blooms in summer/autumn. To keep it small, prune hard back in winter. Alternatively, train up the back wall.

A choice of foliage plants

ABUTILON. A. striatum 'Thompsonii' and the hybrid 'Savitzii' have attractive variegated foliage. Prune back in early spring.

AGLAONEMA. Lush, low-growing evergreen perennials, with silver-speckled or white-variegated foliage. Peat-based compost recommended.

ASPIDISTRA. The cast-iron plant, *A. elatior,* is an evergreen perennial with large, deep green, shiny leaves.

BEGONIA. Large colourful leaves are the attraction of *B.* ×'Cleopatra', *B.* ×'Tiger', *B. masoniana* and *B. rex.* Peat-based compost recommended.

CALADIUM. Caladium bicolor is a perennial with large, multicoloured, paper-thin leaves, which die down in autumn. Keep the plant dry and warm over winter.

CALATHEA. Large, beautifully marked evergreen leaves are the attraction of *C. lancifolia, C. makoyana, C. ornata* and *C. zebrina.*

CODIAEUM. The croton, varieties of *C. variegatum pictum,* have large multicoloured leaves. They are evergreen shrubs.

CORDYLINE. Cordyline terminalis has large evergreen lanceolate leaves, bronzy red or purplish.

CTENANTHE. C. oppenheimiana 'Tricolor' is an evergreen perennial with long leaves marked with white, and bright red on the undersides.

DIEFFENBACHIA. The dumb cane. Evergreen perennials with large leaves, which are heavily patterned

This superb timber-framed building, by Alexander Bartholomew Conservatories Ltd, integrates well with the owners' Japanese rooftop garden, which overlooks the River Thames. Size is 4.8 × 3 m (16 × 10 ft).

with white or cream. Popular kinds are *D. maculata* and *D. exotica*. Do not allow sap to come in contact with mouth or eyes as it causes painful swellings.

DRACAENA. Evergreen shrubs. Popular are *D. deremensis* and its varieties, with green and silver (or white) striped, sword-shaped leaves; and the palm-like *D. marginata*, with long thin leaves.

FERNS. Several ferns are suitable for garden rooms, and make a good foil for brightly coloured pot plants. Try adiantums or maidenhair ferns; *Asplenium bulbiferum*, the spleenwort; *Cyrtomium falcatum*, the holly fern; *Dicksonia antarctica*, the tree fern; *Nephrolepis exaltata*, the sword fern; and *Pteris cretica* and *P. tremula*, the table ferns. Grow in peat-based compost.

FICUS. Apart from the popular rubber plant, *Ficus elastica* 'Decora', there are several other worthwhile species of these evergreen shrubs and trees, including *F. benjamina*, the weeping fig; and *F. lyrata*, the fiddleback fig, with huge spoon-shaped leaves.

GREVILLEA. The silk oak, *Grevillea robusta*, is an evergreen tree with ferny foliage—an ideal foil for brightly coloured plants. Grow in acid compost.

MARANTA. The prayer plant, *M. leuconeura*, is a low-growing evergreen perennial, whose leaves have bluish green veins and purple undersides. Intricately patterned varieties include 'Erythroneura', 'Kerchoveana' and 'Massangeana'. Grow in peat-based compost.

MUSA. Banana plants are grown mainly for their dramatic foliage, and need plenty of space. Try the Canary Island banana, *M. cavendishii*, and *M. ensete*.

PALMS. No garden room is complete without a palm. I recommend larger kinds, like *Howea belmoreana*, *H. forsteriana*, and the Canary Island date palm, *Phoenix canariensis*. In pots these palms will grow to about 1.8–2.4 m (6–8 ft) in height.

PEPEROMIA. The pepper elders are dwarf evergreen perennials. Some have deep green crinkled leaves, like *P. caperata*; others are banded silver and green, such as *P. argyreia*; and there are some with thick fleshy leaves, such as *P. obtusifolia*, 'Green Gold' and 'Variegata' being variegated.

PHILODENDRON. These are essential garden-room foliage plants. Climbing kinds have already been mentioned; shrubby sorts include the well-known *P. bipinnatifidum*, with deeply cut foliage.

SANSEVIERIA. The mother-in-law's tongue, *S. trifasciata* 'Laurentii', has stiff, upright, sword-like leaves edged with yellow. It's a tough, adaptable plant.

YUCCA. *Yucca elephantipes* is an evergreen shrub with a thick trunk, at the top of which is carried a tuft of upright sword-shaped leaves. An ideal 'specimen' plant.

BULBS

A selection of bulbous and tuberous plants can provide colour in the garden room all the year round for a modest outlay.

For spring

Hardy bulbs like hyacinths, daffodils and tulips will provide colour in the cool or unheated garden room in late winter and spring. Try grouping them with other spring-flowering pot plants, such as primulas and cinerarias, and not forgetting some fresh green foliage, such as ferns.

The hardy bulbs are planted in early autumn, generally in bowls, using bulb fibre, with the tips of the bulbs just showing. After planting, they are placed in a cool shady position out of doors and covered with a 15 cm (6 in) layer of peat. They need to be kept in a temperature below 9°C (48°F). After about eight weeks, when roots and shoots have developed, transfer the bulbs to the garden room. After flowering, plant them in the garden.

Alexander Bartholomew Conservatories Ltd supplied this timber-framed, double-glazed, half-octagonal ended building, which blends well with the house.

Inside view of the garden room shown on page 55. Cane furniture is an excellent choice as it blends so well with the plants.

For summer

Summer-flowering bulbs and tubers are started into growth in heat early in the year, after taking a dry winter rest. The tuberous begonias make a highly colourful display with their large double flowers in a wide range of colours. The Indian shot lily, or varieties of *Canna* × *generalis* produce spectacular red, orange or yellow flowers and have large, bold foliage, green or purplish.

The climbing lily, *Gloriosa rothschildiana,* is a climber with crimson and yellow lily-like blooms. The huge trumpet-shaped blooms of hippeastrums make a bold display in the garden room: colours may be crimson, scarlet, pink or white. Various lilies make superb pot plants for the cool garden room, like *Lilium auratum* (white and yellow), 'Enchantment' (orange-red), *L. longiflorum* (white), *L. regale* (white and pink), and *L. speciosum rubrum* (pink and carmine). Pot lilies in autumn, and plant in the garden after flowering.

Gloxinias or sinningias have large bell-shaped blooms in shades of red, pink, purple and white; *Sprekelia formosissima* bears crimson orchid-like blooms; and *Zantedeschia aethiopica,* the arum lily, produces large white spathes. Keep the arum lily moist all year round.

For autumn and winter

Cyclamen are very popular autumn- and winter-flowering pot plants and they can be kept from year to year (dry them off for the summer). Becoming very popular are the miniature varieties, many of which have scented flowers. Freesias are grown mainly for winter flowering and their glorious scent. Plant corms in late summer and treat as for spring bulbs. Dry off the corms for the summer. *Nerine bowdenii* produces pink flowers in autumn. Pot bulbs in late summer, and dry them off and rest them when the leaves die down. *Vallota speciosa,* the Scarborough lily, produces large funnel-shaped scarlet blooms in autumn. Pot bulbs in late summer, and dry them off for the summer, when the leaves start to die down.

CACTI AND SUCCULENTS

The desert cacti and succulents are highly popular plants with owners of garden rooms, and some of the large-growing ones, like the columnar cereus and the branching prickly pears, or opuntia, make dramatic specimens once they have grown to a height of several feet—although this takes many years. It is possible, at a price, of course, to buy fairly large plants from garden centres or specialists.

If you want plenty of flowers, though (the above kinds do not flower until relatively mature, which takes many years), choose some of the smaller cacti which bloom freely when young, like mammillarias, rebutias, notocactus, chamaecereus and ferocactus.

There are many succulents other than cacti, some very popular kinds being agave (the century plant which eventually makes a huge specimen), aloes, crassulas (some of these have a large, branching habit), echeverias, euphorbias (some are large branching plants), lithops or 'living stones', sedums and senecios.

If you have a soil bed in your garden room you could turn it into a 'little desert', by planting a collection of cacti and succulents among a few pieces of natural rock, and covering the soil surface with stone chippings or gravel (Fig. 13).

The desert cacti and succulents need to be kept cool from late autumn to early spring, and warm for the rest of the year. They are ideal plants for the cool garden room. Maximum light is needed, plus sunshine, and dry air. Between late autumn and early spring keep the soil or compost dry; for the rest of the year, when the plants are growing, water regularly when the compost is drying out. Grow plants in a well-drained, gritty compost or soil. Liquid feed plants every three to four weeks in spring and summer.

WATER PLANTS

There are several tender aquatics for the garden-room

Fig. 13 A collection of cacti and succulents grown in a raised bed, edged with natural stone, makes an attractive feature in a garden room. Without the restriction of pots, the plants grow much better and they are easier to look after.

pool, including the tropical waterlilies (*Nymphaea*). For small pools try some of the blue-flowered species like *N. caerulea* and *N. stellata*. Hybrid waterlilies need a largish pool—at least 1.8 by 1.2 m (6 by 4 ft). Try 'General Pershing' (pink), 'Henry Shaw' (blue), 'Missouri' (white), or 'St Louis' (yellow). The sacred lotus, *Nelumbo nucifera,* is similar to waterlilies, needs a large pool and bears rose pink flowers.

In late winter/early spring the tubers of water lilies and lotuses are started into growth. Pot singly into

10 cm (4 in) pots of pure loam and slightly submerge them in a container of water. Provide a temperature of 18–21°C (65–70°F). When the tubers start to form leaves, plant each tuber in a large aquatic basket, using loam. Cover surface with shingle, then place in the pool. Gradually lower the plants in the water as the leaf stalks grow, easily done by standing the baskets on bricks, and removing them as growth increases. A minimum water temperature of 18°C (65°F) is needed. In the autumn remove baskets from pool, allow soil to

This magnificent Edwardian conservatory, constructed *c.* 1905, is built of timber, brick and cast-iron. It measures 6 × 4.2 m (20 × 14 ft).

Inside view of the conservatory shown on page 59. Note the quarry-tiled floor and stone facing to the inside of the walls. The rockery at the far end incorporates a small pool.

dry out, lift the tubers when leaves have died down, and store in moist sand over winter, in a temperature of 13°C (55°F).

Floating aquatics, which are simply dropped into the water, include *Eichhornia crassipes*, the water hyacinth, with rosettes of shiny leaves and pale blue flowers, ideal water temperature 18–21°C (65–70°F), minimum 13°C (55°F); and *Pistia stratiotes*, the water lettuce, with rosettes of pale green leaves, the minimum water temperature needed is 18°C (65°F).

For growing in aquatic baskets in the shallow water at the edge of the pool, try *Cyperus alternifolius*, the umbrella grass, with stiff green stems at the top of which radiate green leafy bracts; and *Zantedeschia aethiopica*, the arum lily, with white spathes in summer.

Submerged oxygenating plants are essential in a pool as they give off oxygen and ensure a well-aerated pool and clear water. Plant in loam in aquatic baskets and place in the bottom of the pool. *Cryptocoryne* needs warm water; there are *Myriophyllum* and *Vallisneria* species, for cool or warm conditions.

ALPINES

To provide colour and interest in the unheated garden room during winter and spring there are few plants to surpass alpines or rock plants, together with miniature hardy bulbs.

Alpines are grown in pans, ideally clay ones, of gritty, soil-based compost: for example, John Innes potting compost No. 1, to which has been added one-third extra coarse sand or grit. The pans of plants are taken into the garden room as they are coming into flower, and for the rest of the year they can be kept in a cold frame, in a sunny spot, covering them with lights only during the winter to keep off excess rain.

Miniature hardy bulbs can be planted in pans of similar compost in early autumn, when they are taken into the garden room. For the rest of the year, after flowering, keep them in the cold frame with the alpines.

Conditions in a garden room displaying alpines and miniature bulbs must be dry and airy, so provide plenty of ventilation and avoid splashing water over plants, staging or floor.

For displaying alpines and miniature bulbs, I suggest a length of deep staging, which can hold about 15 cm (6 in) of pea shingle or gravel, in which the pans can be plunged to their rims.

The most pleasing display is achieved by mixing pans of miniature bulbs with the alpines. You could also have a 'framework' of contrasting woody foliage plants—I particularly recommend dwarf conifers in pots, such as *Juniperus communis* 'Compressa', *Picea albertiana* 'Conica' and *Pinus parviflora brevifolia*.

A choice of alpines

Dianthus alpinus, *Draba aizoides*, *Dryas octopetala*, *Erodium chamaedryoides*, *Gentiana verna*, *Iberis sempervirens*, *Lewisia cotyledon*, *Morisia monanthos*, *Phlox subulata*, *Primula allionii*, *Primula rosea*, *Ranunculus calandrinioides*, *Raoulia australis* (for foliage), *Rhodohypoxis baurii*, *Saxifraga* (*S.* × *apiculata*, *S.* × *burseriana*, *S.* × *elizabethae*, *S.* × *jenkinsae*, *S.* 'Southside Seedling'), *Sedum spathulifolium* 'Purpureum' (for foliage), and *Sempervivum* (many species, for foliage).

A choice of miniature bulbs

Anemone blanda, *Chionodoxa luciliae*, *Crocus* (*C. ancyrensis*, *C. chrysanthus* cultivars, *C. imperati*, *C. laevigatus*), *Cyclamen coum hiemale*, *Eranthis* (*E. hyemalis*, *E.* × *tubergenii*), *Galanthus* (*G. byzantinus*, *G. corcyrensis*, *G. ikariae*, *G. nivalis*), *Iris* (*I. danfordiae*, *I. histrioides major*, *I. reticulata*), *Muscari armeniacum*, *Narcissus* (*N. asturiensis* syn. *N. minimus*, *N. bulbocodium*, *N. cyclamineus*, *N. juncifolius*), *Scilla* (*S. bifolia*, *S. sibirica*, *S. tubergeniana*), *Tulipa* (*T. humilis*, *T. kaufmanniana* cultivars, *T. pulchella* and *T. tarda*).

8

THE PRODUCTIVE GARDEN ROOM

Various fruits are traditionally grown in the garden room and not only do they provide refreshing desserts for the table but are also attractive in themselves. Luscious bunches of grapes; the flowers and ripening fruits of peaches, nectarines and citrus; and the fruits and foliage of figs can hardly be considered dull or uninteresting.

Fruits can be further enhanced by growing them in white wooden tubs or large terracotta pots of classical design. Containers at least 60 cm (24 in) in diameter and depth will eventually be needed by fruiting plants. The alternative is to grow them in a soil bed—but not for figs as they would make excessive growth; better to confine these to pots.

GRAPE VINES

Grape vines (*Vitis vinifera*) can be grown in a cool or unheated garden room. Popular varieties are 'Black Hamburgh' (black), and 'Buckland Sweetwater' (white).

Traditionally a grape vine is grown on the back wall and you should provide a system of horizontal wires, spaced 30 cm (12 in) apart, up the wall and into the roof area. Space vines 1.2 m (4 ft) apart, planting in fertile soil or soil-based potting compost. Prune back to 60 cm (24 in) after planting.

Side shoots produced from the young rod have their tips cut out when 60 cm (24 in) long. In the following winter they are pruned back to within one growth bud of their base. Also cut back the main rod to well-ripened wood.

In the second year the new side shoots produced in spring are trained horizontally to the wires, but don't allow the vine to fruit. Stop side shoots before they become too long. In the second and subsequent years winter pruning consists of cutting back all side shoots to within one or two growth buds of their base.

After the second year one can allow two bunches of grapes to develop on each side shoot. Hand pollinate flowers by drawing your half-closed hand down each truss. Berries must be thinned out with fine-tipped scissors, especially those in the centre of each bunch.

Cut out side shoots at two leaves beyond a bunch of fruits. Cut back sublateral shoots to one leaf.

In warm conditions vines like humidity, except when in flower and in fruit. Water well in growing season, but keep only slightly moist when the vine is resting in winter. Feed with a vine or general purpose fertilizer in summer.

FIGS

Figs (*Ficus carica*) are suitable for the cool garden room and are grown in large pots or tubs as bush trees. Good varieties are 'Brown Turkey', 'Brunswick' and 'White Marseilles'.

Pot a young fig in late autumn, ensuring plenty of drainage material in the bottom, and using well-firmed John Innes potting compost No. 2 or 3.

Regular pruning will be necessary. Fruits are produced only on new growth and they start forming in the autumn, with more appearing in spring. These should give you two crops per year. Prune in summer

This magnificent modular timber/brick garden room was supplied by Room Outside Ltd. The interior 'atmosphere' is extended on to the terrace by careful choice of plants.

by shortening any vigorous new shoots to five or six leaves from their base. Thin out older branches if they are becoming congested. Aim to encourage a succession of new shoots which will bear fruits. Remove any weak or spindly growth.

Plants do not need shade, but like humidity in warm conditions. The plants rest in winter, when the compost is kept only barely moist. Water well in growing period.

PEACHES AND NECTARINES

Peaches and nectarines (*Prunus persica*), are ideal for the unheated garden room and are grown in the same way. Good peach varieties include 'Bellegarde', 'Dymond', 'Hale's Early', 'Peregrine', and 'Royal George'; and recommended nectarines are 'Early Rivers', 'Lord Napier' and 'Pine Apple'.

They can be trained to a fan shape on the back wall. For each tree you will need wall space of at least 1.8 by 1.8 m (6 by 6 ft). Plant in a soil bed or tub and put up horizontal wires for training, spaced 20 cm (8 in) apart. Plant two-year-old fan-trained trees in late autumn or winter. Then prune hard, by cutting back the middle branch (which is growing vertically) to the topmost pair of side branches. The two side branches are then cut back lightly and tied in to one of the wires. Prune back any remaining branches to within a few centimetres of the main stem.

In spring many new shoots will be produced and must be thinned out, by rubbing them out with finger and thumb. Leave only sufficient to form a fan-shaped system of main branches. Tie them in as they grow.

By the second winter the main branches should have produced several shoots along their length and made extension growth. Some shoots may have produced flower buds and you can allow a few fruits to develop. Tie in the shoots as flat as possible.

Apart from this basic method of training, peaches and nectarines also need annual pruning in winter.

Shoots which have carried fruits (and which are produced on the main framework of branches) are pruned back to new shoots. These replace the ones cut back and will carry fruits in the following summer. There is a constant succession of fruiting shoots.

The trees rest between late autumn and late winter when they should be kept only slightly moist. The trees like humidity during warm conditions of spring and summer, except during fruit ripening. Hand pollinate the flowers by dabbing each in turn with a soft artist's brush. Thin out new shoots as necessary in spring and summer to avoid congestion (a great many are produced) but leave sufficient for fruiting next year. The fruitlets will need thinning—leave two or three on each shoot. Feed with a high-potash fertilizer in summer.

CITRUS FRUITS

Oranges and lemons are suitable for the intermediate garden room and make excellent tub plants. They are evergreen spiny shrubs and produce fragrant flowers. Among the oranges available are *Citrus aurantium*, the Seville or sour orange; *C. reticulata*, the mandarin or tangerine; and *C. sinensis*, the sweet orange, of which there are many varieties, these being the oranges we buy in the shops.

The lemon is *C. limon*, and the grapefruit *C. × paradisi*.

Young plants should be potted on until they are eventually in large pots or tubs. Use John Innes potting compost No. 3. Pot on during winter.

Keep only slightly moist in winter but water freely during the rest of the year. Humidity is enjoyed in warm conditions. Plants can be stood out of doors during the summer in a sunny spot. Plenty of warmth is needed in the growing season to encourage fruits to mature.

Citrus do not need regular pruning but light pruning can be carried out every two or three years to keep the plants shapely. Shoots can be shortened by up to two-thirds. Prune in early spring.

Bougainvillea (*top, centre*), streptocarpus (*bottom, centre*), pelargoniums and a wealth of foliage plants provide summer colour in this garden room.

A warm garden room is a haven for sumptuous tropical plants, like the yellow-flowered *Aphelandra squarrosa* 'Louisae', and foliage plants like coloured-leaved codiaeums and green-leaved aglaonemas.

9

KEEPING PLANTS HEALTHY

In the chapters dealing with plants, I have purposely given very little in the way of cultural advice, simply because it is repetitive—the majority of plants needing the same conditions, care etc. Temperature ranges, though, have been given in Chapter 6. However, where cultivation differs from the norm—for example, as with cacti and succulents—I have given sufficient detail in the appropriate places. Here, general cultivation of garden-room plants is considered, and applies to all plants mentioned, unless otherwise stated in the other chapters.

HUMIDITY

Humidity is the amount of moisture in the air and it is important to provide the correct level for garden-room plants. It is measured as Relative Humidity (RH), on a scale 0 to 100. On this scale, RH 0% is completely dry air; at the other extreme, RH 100%, the air is saturated with water.

Humidity can be measured with a hygrometer or 'moisture meter'. Sometimes this is combined with a thermometer.

Some of the plants mentioned prefer quite a dry atmosphere, like the desert cacti and succulents, pelargoniums, sansevierias, yuccas, chrysanthemums and hardy annuals. However, the majority of plants like a humid atmosphere. But how much humidity is actually needed? For desert cacti and succulents, and other plants which need a dryish atmosphere, RH 35–40% is about right. Average garden-room plants will be happy if the RH is around 60%. However, there are some plants (thin-leaved or very delicate tropical kinds, like caladiums) which relish RH of around 80%, but this cannot be maintained in a garden room which is to be occupied by people.

As a general rule to follow, the lower the temperature in the garden room, the drier the air must be. So in an unheated or cool garden room during the autumn and winter the air must be kept very dry. In warmer conditions the humidity should be higher.

Of course, in a garden room used as a living area we cannot maintain jungle-like conditions as this would be unbearable for us. Instead, we have to provide humidity immediately around the plants—localize it. This can be achieved in several ways.

Potted plants can be stood on shallow trays filled with gravel, shingle or one of the horticultural aggregates. These materials are kept moist to create a humid atmosphere around the plants, but make sure the pots do not stand in water or the compost will become too wet.

Another method, which I have mentioned on p.36, is to place pots in ornamental pot holders, or groups of plants in larger containers, and to fill the space up to the pot rim with peat or horticultural aggregate, which again should be kept moist.

Another method of ensuring humid conditions around plants is to spray them daily or twice daily in warm conditions with plain water, using a mist sprayer. However, do not spray flowers, plants with hairy or woolly leaves, or cacti and succulents. It is best to use soft water or rainwater for spraying plants, for hard or alkaline water can result in unsightly white marks on the leaves.

SHADING

Adequate shading is needed by both plants and people in the spring and summer. Without shading the leaves and flowers of most plants can be badly scorched during periods of strong sunshine. Shading also helps to keep the temperatures down to an acceptable level in hot weather.

For plants, shading should ideally only be used when the sun is shining, and removed during dull periods so that they receive maximum light, and this is best achieved by using roller blinds. During autumn and winter shading is not needed in the UK—certainly plants need all the light available during these seasons.

It should be borne in mind, however, that some garden-room plants like plenty of sun for healthy growth. Of the plants mentioned in this book the following come in this category: *Callistemon, Cassia, Lantana, Nerium, Bougainvillea, Chrysanthemum, Pelargonium, Sansevieria, Nerine, Citrus,* peaches and nectarines, *Punica, Tropaeolum,* cacti and succulents, *Yucca* and figs.

For the sake of convenience it would perhaps be better to grow in your garden room only plants which need to be shaded—that is, if it is used as a living area. Alternatively, grow any sun-lovers in their own special corner which can be left unshaded.

VENTILATION

Plants as well as people need fresh air at all times and therefore adequate ventilation is needed all the year round. Ventilation also helps to reduce the temperature, particularly necessary in hot weather; and it helps to reduce humidity, which is important for plants growing in unheated or cool conditions. So even in the unheated or cool garden room in winter, ventilation is needed.

However, the amount of ventilation you provide should be consistent with maintaining the desired temperature—there is no point in providing a great deal of ventilation if it results in the temperature dropping to an uncomfortable level for plants and people.

The way to ensure effective ventilation is to open the roof ventilators and also the side ventilators or louvres. The warm air rises and escapes through the roof, sucking in cool air through the side ventilators. Extractor fans achieve the same effect.

WATERING

As a general rule, plants need more water in the growing season, from mid-spring to early autumn, and far less during the rest of the year, when they are making little growth or are completely resting. Plants which drop their leaves in the autumn, and take a complete rest, should be kept only slightly moist, or even completely dry in the case of many bulbs, corms and tubers. Desert cacti and succulents are kept dry between late autumn and early spring.

But how do we know when to water in the growing season? Bear in mind that we do not want the compost to dry out too much during this period. I would advise testing the compost for moisture with a finger. Press a finger into the surface and if it feels dry on top, but moist below, then apply water. If the surface is moist, or even wet, do not water. When watering do not give a 'quick splash', but fill the space between the compost surface and the rim of the pot with water. This will ensure the compost is moistened right the way down to the bottom of the pot.

A soil bed or border can be tested in the same way: apply sufficient water to penetrate to a depth of about 15cm (6in), which means giving about 27 l/sqm (4¾gal/sqyd).

When watering between early autumn and mid-spring, during the plants' rest period, and when conditions are cooler, the compost or soil should be kept only slightly moist (except for plants which are dried off completely), so one has to water very sparingly. How can we put this into practice? Again I would advise testing with a finger, pushing it well down into the compost. If the compost is dry on the surface, and feels dryish but not completely dry lower down, water

A warm garden room, with tropical ferns under the staging and, on top, foliage plants like silvery *Fittonia argyroneura*, purple-spotted maranta (*foreground*), *Ficus benjamina,* dizygotheca, peperomias, *Rhoeo discolor minima,* and *Pseuderanthemum reticulatum.*

can be applied, again filling the space between the compost surface and the rim of the pot. Then leave well alone until the compost is drying out again. If in doubt, it is far better not to water than to keep the compost too wet. Far better to leave the plant for a few more days, unless it is wilting.

If you do not want to use your fingers for testing compost or soil, buy a soil-moisture meter, which consists of a metal probe with a calibrated dial at the top. The dial indicates the state of the soil: 'dry', 'moist' and 'wet'.

It probably goes without saying that in cold or cool conditions the compost or soil dries out far more slowly than in warm conditions. In a warm garden room you will be watering more often than in a cool or cold building.

FEEDING

Potting composts supply plants with foods for a certain period, generally several months, depending on the type of fertilizer used in the mix, so newly potted plants do not need feeding. The time to start is when the roots have permeated the new compost, which in practical terms is about two months. The same applies to plants which have been potted on to larger pots.

Then feeding can be carried out about once a fortnight, but only in the growing season, from mid-spring to early autumn. Do not feed at any other time as plants are resting and will not make use of any fertilizer applied: an excess of foods can build up, which can be harmful.

There are various ways of feeding potted plants, but the most popular is to apply a liquid fertilizer. There are many proprietary brands available, but for garden-room plants I would suggest using a house-plant fertilizer, some of which are based on seaweed. It is possible to buy fertilizers specially for flowering houseplants, and fertilizers which have been formulated for foliage plants.

Another way of feeding plants in pots is to use fertilizer tablets, again specially formulated for house-

plants. These are about the size of an aspirin tablet and are simply pushed into the compost, where they release plant foods over a period of weeks. Fertilizer sticks work in the same way.

There are various ways, too, of feeding permanent plants in soil beds or borders. I like to apply a dry general purpose fertilizer in mid-spring and lightly prick it into the soil surface. Then in the summer, if I feel that plants need a boost, I water them with a general purpose liquid fertilizer, say about once a month. Plants in soil beds do not need feeding as regularly as potted plants, as foods are not leached out so rapidly.

Plants should not be fed if the compost or soil is dry—water it first and then feed when the plants are fully charged with water. It is most important to apply fertilizers strictly according to the instructions on the packet or bottle, for you could harm plants by applying too much, or too strong a solution.

COMPOSTS, SOILS AND POTTING

The majority of plants make much better growth if they are potted on regularly into larger pots. If allowed to become pot-bound, when the compost is tightly packed with roots, growth will slow down considerably. The compost will also dry out very rapidly so you will be forever watering, and there is the risk plants will suffer stress from lack of moisture.

The majority of garden room plants can be safely potted on in mid-spring; it is best to avoid potting on during resting periods.

To ascertain whether or not a plant needs potting on, you will need to inspect the roots. To do this, turn the pot upside down and tap the rim on the edge of a table or bench to loosen the rootball, and slide off the pot (Fig. 14). If there is a mass of roots then pot on; but if a large volume of the compost has no roots through it, return the plant to its present pot.

If possible pot on to the next size of pot, for example

Bougainvillea 'Miss Manila Hybrid' supported on a timber and brick pergola. The idea could be scaled down in a smaller garden room.

A brick pillar provides support for *Mandevilla boliviensis,* while *Acalypha wilkesiana roseomarginata* provides a purple background for pot plants, which include lilac and purple streptocarpus, orange aeschynanthus, red and yellow iresine, red-flowered hibiscus and *Asparagus densiflorus* 'Sprengeri'.

By far the most attractive and easiest way of growing epiphytic bromeliads is on a section of tree or tree branch. The pot-grown bromeliads have been plunged in a layer of pine needles to enhance the display.

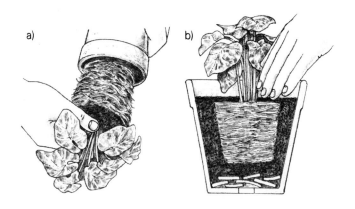

a) b)

Fig. 14 To ensure steady and healthy growth most conservatory plants need potting quite regularly into larger pots. This should normally be done before the present pot is tightly packed with roots, so periodic checking of the rootball will be necessary (*a*). If the plant needs moving on (*b*), either put it into the next size of pot or move it on two sizes. There should not be a large volume of compost around the roots or this will remain very wet and could lead to root rot. When we come on to larger pots—say over 15 cm (6 in) in diameter, it is advisable to use drainage material in the bottom, such as a layer of broken clay flower pots or 'crocks'.

from a 13 cm (5 in) pot to a 15 cm (6 in) pot. However, more vigorous plants can with advantage be moved on two sizes—for instance, from a 10 cm (4 in) pot to a 15 cm (6 in) pot. I have suggested that many garden-room plants which eventually become quite large can be grown in large pots, tubs etc. It is best not to plant small young plants direct into large containers as they will have too much compost around the roots, which is liable to remain wet. Instead, pot on as suggested above. When the plants are in quite large—say 20 cm (8 in)—pots then they could be planted into tubs or very large pots—30 cm (12 in) diameter and upwards.

Drainage material is needed for pots over 15 cm (6 in) in diameter. The traditional drainage material is broken clay flower pots, known as 'crocks'. A large piece is placed over the drainage hole and then a layer of smaller pieces placed over this. Cover with a thin layer of rough peat or leafmould, followed by a layer of compost which should be firmed. Place the plant in

the centre and fill in with compost, firming all round with your fingers. You should ensure the top of the rootball is slightly covered with fresh compost, and there must be space between the final compost level and the rim of the pot, to allow room for watering. This can be about 12 mm ($\frac{1}{2}$ in) for small pots, and 2.5 cm (1 in) and more for larger pots and tubs.

After potting water in the plant with a rosed watering can to settle the compost around the roots.

Plastic pots are often used today, but for plants which like very well-drained conditions and dryish compost, such as desert cacti and succulents, I prefer clay pots. I also use clay pots for larger plants as they are heavier and more stable.

Large plants which are in their final large pots or tubs will from time to time need a fresh supply of compost. This is achieved by the technique known as re-potting. It can be carried out in mid-spring, or in winter for dormant plants like the fruits and deciduous shrubs.

Re-potting is recommended every two years. First remove the plant from its container. In the case of large specimens, two people may be needed to accomplish this. Place the container on its side, and while one person gently but firmly pulls the plant, the other person firmly taps the rim of the container with a brick or large block of wood. Hopefully, the rootball will then slide out! If not insert a long blade between the inside edge of the container and the rootball, and work it all round.

Then about 5 cm (2 in) of old compost is teased away from all round the rootball, and from the bottom and top. At the same time, roots can be trimmed back by this amount. Then replace the plant in its container (which should have been thoroughly cleaned out and dried). Work fresh compost between the rootball and sides of container.

In the years between re-potting, fresh compost can be added at the top, first scraping away about 5 cm (2 in) of the old compost.

Now let us take a look at suitable potting composts. It is safe to say that all garden-room plants will thrive in soil-based, the traditional John Innes, compost, and

In this temperate or coolish garden room summer colour is provided by trained bougainvilleas (*foreground*), large coleus for coloured foliage, streptocarpus, and golden-leaved helxine. At the back of the group *Grevillea robusta* provides fresh ferny foliage.

75

An attractive grouping of tropical plants in a warm garden room. In the foreground is *Ctenanthe oppenheimiana* 'Tricolor'. The blue flowers belong to *Dichorisandra reginae*. The plants in the background include coloured-leaved codiaeums and cordylines.

Summer colour in a temperate or coolish garden room: pink and purple streptocarpus hybrids, *Kohleria eriantha* (orange flowers), *Whitfieldia elongata* (white flowers), *Hedera helix* 'Goldheart' and trailing, variegated *Callisia repens*.

this is certainly recommended for plants in larger containers. For the initial potting of young plants, such as seedlings and rooted cuttings, use John Innes potting compost No. 1. When potting on use No. 2 which contains twice the amount of fertilizer. For potting on large plants—for instance, shrubs and fruits which are being grown in large pots or tubs—use No. 3 (which contains three times the amount of fertilizer).

Many garden-room plants, except desert kinds such as cacti and succulents, can also be grown in the more modern soilless or peat-based composts, formulated for houseplants or general purpose use. Do not grow large plants in these, though, for they will not keep the plants sufficiently stable. It is best to stick to one type of compost throughout the life of the plant—in other words, do not transfer a plant from soil-based to peat-based compost, or *vice versa*. Follow the manufacturer's instructions when using soilless composts, as they do not need much firming.

If you are making up soil beds, you can use either good-quality topsoil, such as a light or medium loam, or John Innes potting compost No. 2 or 3.

Bear in mind that some plants need acid or lime-free compost (indicated where appropriate), so for these use one of the proprietary ericaceous composts.

PESTS AND DISEASES

An aerosol houseplant pest killer with a wide spectrum of activity will eradicate pests like greenfly, red spider mites, whitefly, scale insects, mealy bugs and thrips.

To date there are no fungicides specifically for use in the home, so if any of your plants are infected with common fungal diseases such as mildew and grey mould (botrytis), then take them out in the garden and spray them thoroughly with benomyl fungicide. When dry take them back inside.

Control of the two most serious garden-room pests—whitefly and red spider mites—can be even more effectively achieved by means of biological control. Predatory or parasitic insects are introduced which prey on the pests. They are supplied on leaves from specialist producers and the leaves are placed among the plants. A good time to commence biological control is in early or mid-spring.

Introduce parasites or predators only when pests are found on the plants otherwise they will not survive because they will have nothing to live on—they do not feed on plants. And do not use insecticides with biological control or you will kill the beneficial creatures.

Red spider mites are controlled with the predatory mite *Phytoseiulus persimilis* and whitefly with the parasitic wasp *Encarsia formosa*.

Mealy bugs and scale insects are also the bane of the garden-room owner's life, and are often found on woody plants, as well as on others, like cacti and succulents. Although tedious, I have found that an effective method of control is to dab each one with a soft brush dipped in methylated spirit.

INDEX